Observations from the Writer's Chair

Joseph J. Gombita

To Pearl.
with love,
Joe Gombita

Observations from the Writer's Chair

For my family and friends, with love

I would like to thank my best friend, JJ Marconi, who took the time to provide his excellent photography skills for the cover. You're the best, man.

CONTENTS

PART II: GROWING UP

PART V: LOSS

PART VI: IDOL

PART VII: FORWARD

PREFACE

I am surprised I have not wrecked my car yet! I say this with a smirk on my face because I cannot begin to count how many times, while sitting at a red light, I pulled out paper and a pen and began jotting down words and phrases of something that has inspired me at that moment. When something came to mind, I had to write it down, even if that meant nearly causing an accident. Whether it was seeing a person walking down the street or a song that came on the radio, I took inspiration from all aspects of everyday life.

I have a strict ritual when writing poetry; I put on music, light candles, and let the genius in me come to life. That seems a bit egotistical; however, that process works best for me. Most of the time, I end up awake until two in the morning because my struggle comes with the last line or two of a poem. By then, I am ready to throw the thing away. Finally, inspiration hits as I am shutting my computer off. While writing, I enjoy the music of Elton John and Billy Joel. Although they write in completely different styles, it is the emotion, personality and storytelling in their lyrics that capture me.

These poems have been in the making for several years. Each of them was written in a unique way. Whether it was while driving in the car or on vacation at the beautiful beaches of North Carolina, I absorbed the world around me and wrote it down on paper. Writing poetry is a religious experience. Now, I am not a religious person by any stretch of the imagination; however, there are so many beautiful and dark mysteries in this world that inspire me. I am not a very outspoken person; however, I usually find my voice somewhere in my poetry. No matter my reasons or what has inspired me over the years, my place and my meaning are carved into the following pages. From my childhood to the very second that I am writing this preface, I am still evolving as a writer, and I cannot say when I will be finished. I believe that in order to write poetry, one must have something important to say. When there is nothing left to say, there is nothing more to be written. But for now, I am still writing. Anyway, writing has always been a drug for me, an *obsession*. Just the idea of pouring my emotions onto paper gives me such a satisfying and euphoric feeling each time. But no matter what life experiences have created this madness, these poems shone light on the darkness every time. I would like to say that writing these poems has shaped my life in some crazy way.

Joseph J. Gombita

Part I

The Writer's Chair

Untitled

Poetry is a window into the soul:
The darkness,
The mystery,
The sadness
And the pain,
But to understand it, you have to read between the lines,
And then you'll see through the window,
Into the room that is my life.

In The Middle of the Night

In the middle of the night,
I dream about the other side,
Beyond this darkness,
Where a different light shines,
I'm drowning in this darkness
Taking over my life,
Something deep inside of me
That's been hard to find,
Something I don't understand
'Cause it's been hard to define.

In the middle of the night,
I wander through my dreams,
Searching for a sign
That's deep inside of me,
I don't think I'm happy,
I don't think I ever was,
Sometimes I lie in bed with my eyes closed
And wonder too much,
Searching for an answer
That never was.

And I don't need your prayer,
I just need a different light
To shine out of the darkness
That is my life,
Don't need a cross, don't need a sign
To show me everything I've sacrificed
In the middle of the night

Behind my weary eyes I dream
About a different life,
One that I once knew,

One that wasn't hard to define,
But something keeps me here
And I can't break free,
I'm drowning in this darkness
That's taking over me.

And I don't need a black book
I just need a different light
To shine out of the darkness
That is my life,
Don't need a cross, don't need a sign
To show me everything I've sacrificed,
In the middle of the night
In the middle of the night

On The Outside Looking In

Late one evening
The rain began to fall
And the manikins come to life
Somewhere down the hall,
Oh, it shows,
My creativity,
And the manikins come to life
Somewhere down the hall

Blank empty stares,
Static on the telephone,
Seven billion people
And no one's home,
Oh, it shows,
My brilliance:
Seven billion people
And I'm all alone.

Wish I could have stopped the change,
Wish I could have stopped the rain,
But I left my umbrella at home,
My forgetfulness shows,
I'm on the outside looking in,
What I see is what I get.

Sitting by the fire,
Watching it snow,
Getting cold in here
But nobody knows,
Oh, it shows,
My stamina,
It's getting cold in here
But nobody knows,

It's getting cold in here
But nobody knows.

If These Walls Could Talk

There's a note that I wrote crumbled up on the floor,
And there's a chair pushed up against the door,
No more tears is no more pain,
No more suffering is letting go of yesterday.

If these walls could talk, they'd say I'm alone,
And they'd say that I haven't far to go
Until I see the other side of the cold, dark night
Filled with the catastrophes of an imperfect life

In every corner of the room
My hell survives,
And an unfinished prayer echoes for you
Filled with the love I could never prove,
In every corner of the room
My darkness hides,
And an unfinished letter waits for you
Filled with the love I could never prove.

My shaky hands can't hold the gun still,
And there's a childproof cap
Keeping me from the pills,
Suddenly I see the monster I've become
And he's the one holding the gun.

In every corner of the room
My hell survives,
And an unfinished prayer echoes for you
Filled with the love I could never prove,
In every corner of the room
My darkness hides
And an unfinished letter waits for you
Filled with the love I could never prove.

The noose feels so cold against my virgin skin,
Holding me like my mother never did when I was a kid,
The thought of falling into the darkness for just one second tonight
Holds me close and it holds me tight.

Oh, the very thought of falling into the darkness for just one second
tonight
Holds me close and it holds me right.

Pain

This world's so cold,
Shades of grey are all I see anymore,
Peace crawls
And war builds a wall
Between us all,
This world's so cold.

It's plain to see
That mankind's diseased,
Prayer stalls
And religion builds a wall
Between us all,
Oh, it divides
Different lives,
But somewhere in between
The money hungry
Bigot sleeps.

This world's so cold,
Shades of grey are all I see anymore,
Love is blind
And hard to find
In anyone, anymore,
This world's so cold.

Money talks, money talks a lot,
And government lies,
They deceive, they mislead,
This world's so damn cold to me.

Money talks, money talks a lot,
But love doesn't cost a thing,
Peace is cheap, peace is free,

This world's so damn cold to me.

Faith divides
And churches give believers
Some place to hide,
Hell is free,
Heaven isn't cheap,
This world's so damn cold to me.

Vagabond Heart

I'm sitting in my hotel room
Waiting for my room service to arrive,
Well, it's nine o'clock
At night,
Mine's the only car sitting in the parking lot,
Such an easy life for a vagabond,
Well, I'm going down to the bar
But no one's there,
So, I guess I'll just sit here
And stare into the empty air.

I'm surfing through the channels
But nothing's on,
The lobby's silent,
Everybody's gone,
My tab's still open at the hotel bar,
I'm drifting in and out of consciousness,
But the bartender,
He's got a really big heart,
Listening to me spill my guts
About my recent streak of bad luck,
Quite frankly,
I think I'm losing my touch.

My cavalier attitude
Gets me into trouble sometimes,
I put on a show
Just so you can watch me lose my mind,
Me, I'm just falling apart,
Sipping my gin and tonic
At the hotel bar,
Pouring my thoughts on you,
Unwrapping my entire life,

It's such a complex life for a
Vagabond

I'm such a fool for losing my cool,
Letting my life come undone
At the seams,
It's such a calamity,
Well, my tab's closed at the bar,
Such a sad life for a
Vagabond

Well, I'm going back to my hotel room,
Waiting for the morning to arrive,
The lobby's empty,
Everybody's gone,
It's such a lonely life for a vagabond.

This Dirty Water

I'm standing on a bridge watching the water pass beneath,
And I'm confused because I don't know what it means,
This delusion hits me every time I sit down to write,
So I throw some wood together that'll get me to the other side,
But it's been raining here for days, water's running high,
And I've been stuck on this rock trying to find a sign,
Those critics, they tell me they want a song written soon,
But there are only so many words I can write by noon.

Oh, and this dirty water slowly poisons my soul,
But the fight of the rapids makes this steam ship
Feel like she's old,
And sometimes the water's deep, coming up over my head,
And before I can swim, the water rises up again,
'Cause the rapids are so much stronger
And I'm drowning in this dirty water,
It feels like a curse every time I try to write a verse,
'Cause the rapids are so much stronger
And I'm going down in this dirty water.

There's candlelight in the widow up in the room on the left,
That light's all that's left inside my weary head,
'Cause I never knew the rapids would grow stronger,
The wrath of this dirty water
Shouldn't last much longer,
Oh, there's a bird in the tree watching me through the rain
That's coming down in sheets making the water rise again.

No matter how high the water gets,
The rapids will always be stronger,
The water won't stay high forever,
But I'm drowning in this dirty water.

Downeaster

Waves crash along the shore of an eroded beach,
Slowly his memories are becoming out of reach,
And tomorrow is today
And today is yesterday,
But behind closed eyes, such a fantastic life,
With no more color,
Now his memories are only in black and white.

Storm clouds gather on the bay
As the old boat captain readies his Downeaster
To sail away,
He lights a cigar and pours himself a glass of wine
And tries real hard to remember a better time,
Turning the ship's wheel, he heads into the storm,
Puts on his jacket, he's trying to keep warm,
Lightning scatters across an unforgiving sky,
Rain drops collect in the storm drain
He calls life.

The old boat captain slowly turns his ship to face the wind,
There's no marlin to be caught in rough seas like this,
A voice full of prayer, broken rosaries,
He's left in the hands of God
And the monster out at sea,
"The storm's only gonna get worse from here,"
But he heads farther into the storm
'Cause there's nothing left to fear,
He holds a picture of his wife
Close to his heart,
He smiles and closes his eyes
And thanks God for letting him come this far,
Memories of his wife, his kids, have begun to fade,
He comes to realize *tomorrow* is today.

The storm now cleared, water's calm as glass,
The old man and his vessel have
Found serenity at last,
I guess that old man kept true to what he did:
He never stopped working,
At least he never thought he did.

In my lifetime, I have seen the sadness and despair that Dementia causes. Watching people suffer through this hellish disease provided the inspiration for "Downeaster." So many souls tormented, day after day, by this horrible disease.

Vintage

Standing against the wall, a four foot tall old vintage mirror with a past that walks,
Standing inside it, a man who looks like me,
But he's much younger like I used to be,
My mind's becoming fragile, who am I today?
Nothing's as it seems, everything has changed,
But something in my mind sticks like glue,
Fragments of my life slowly coming loose,
I wasn't a hero, just somebody who had a job and made a living,
Somebody with some place to go,
But those days are gone, left to die along some abandoned road.

A cup of coffee and a few pills are keeping me alive against my will,
But as I walk past my old vintage mirror,
I still see that young man standing there,
He must've been a pharmacist at one time,
Someone, who made a living, earning his dime,
But time's just a piece of string
And it's fraying fast, ready to lose everything,
How I'd love to go back home to the place that I once knew,
But now it's just a memory slowly fading too.

Standing against the wall, a four foot tall old vintage mirror with a past that walks,
And I can see a young man, someone like me,
He must've been important,
Dressed in a white coat, he must've been a pharmacist,
But he sure looks good to me,
I just wish I could recall anything at all,
I'm breaking down; this old engine's beginning to stall,
This place is a living hell!
And I'm just an old book collecting dust on its shelves,
Haven't read that thing in years,

I'd only be getting it wet with my tears,
Heard it was a bestseller at one time,
Now it only reads the line
...once upon a time

It seems my vintage days are fading fast,
Just a fragment of my life I thought would last,
No matter my state, my reflection's remained the same,
Seems I'm getting older but who I am will never change.

Animals

Wild, willing and wonderful,
A city of animals comes out to play,
In the city no one notices
How many aren't taken care,
The world outside suffers
While we're here where they love us
And keep us safe,
All warm and nice, our blinders are on,
'Cause we ignore the weak and acknowledge the strong,
Don't care if we're right or wrong
We think so high and mighty of ourselves,
But some still cry because they need help,
In a world that is ignorantly blind,
Yes, we're animals
And we're viciously kind.

Made In The USA

I was made from the sins of my father and the love of my mother,
I was bruised and battered: I needed a brother,
Someone who'd love me
And could show some muscle.

I was made from your hopes and dreams,
But something came apart at the seams,
It was something that you just couldn't see,
We prayed to God but we never believed.

I was made from the stars and stripes,
You know, the flag they wave in foreign eyes,
They stirred up a battle and told me to fight,
So I cocked my gun because I thought it was right.

It's been hard to hide our history, such a scandalous country,
It comes with the job but it doesn't pay
Being made in the USA

Yeah, it's been hard to hide our history, such a scandalous country,
It comes with the job but it doesn't pay
Being made in the USA

But no matter what this says,
It's so much more than you think,
It comes with the job but it doesn't pay
Being made in the USA

America the Beautiful

So much division in this landscape,
White man wears his pride,
He takes this land by force
And only gives disease to the tribes,
But he builds a railroad
And connects two broken sides,
He stands on a mountaintop
And claims the great divide

So much heartache
Paints these iron fences,
Painted from the blood of the stolen
And the blood of the taken,
White man's gonna crumble,
It's only a matter of time,
Wild horses will someday
Rein free from these iron fences.

The river that brought us here
Has become dry as a bone,
Freedom used to reign here
But freedom reigns here no more,
"America the beautiful," never made much sense to me,
It was never as beautiful as they made it out to be.

So much pain
Hidden behind these walls:
Documents signed
And legislation
Have left us all to fall,
But we keep our helmets on
Because America is strong
And America is beautiful,

Beautifully wrong

Blood and Tears

The spirit of the sun warms the land today,
Quiet is the frontier, nothing but the wind in your way,
No grease on the river, water blue as the summer's sky,
But prejudice hides in the white man's mind.

White man worries none: skips you like stones on a creek,
Breaks you like a twig and mocks your beliefs,
Sacred land, no more sacred than it should be,
They swallow you whole and you can't breathe.

Though you know the land better than I,
There's no place your people can hide,
White man moving west casts a spell on you
And there ain't a damn thing you can do.

Disease hides in the quilts given to you out of bluffed guilt,
White man stands before you, sets fire to the village you built,
Better get down on your bloody knees
And embrace the white man's philosophy.

Stranger in a Strange Land

A message in a bottle
Filled with sand and glue,
Stuck together is direction
And a little dirty truth,
Sacred stones lie along the beach,
Civilization grows farther out of reach
Away from me

My boat lies in ruins,
Hot sun like a big red flare,
"Build me a fire"
I ask the gods standing there,
A reckless human being
Ignorant of his instinctual ways,
But you say I'm not much further
From an animal locked in a crate.

I know not what they say
Nor do I understand their faith,
But I won't try to understand,
I'm a stranger in a strange land.

Building sculptures in the sand
reminds me of home,
How far away am I?
This I'll never know,
Sticks and stones make up their homes,
Gods drawn on the wall,
Standing before us all
Some things I don't understand,
I'm a stranger in a strange land.

They're not like me,

So much taller than I,
Before me is a parallel that I try to understand,
But I'm a stranger in a strange land.

Morning Mr. President

I've made friends,
Made enemies,
Seen the world turn its head away from me,
But I don't care
Because I'm still standing here,
Gonna take a lot to bring me down,
Not calling myself God
But I'm the second biggest thing in town.

Guess I'm the biggest thing since sliced bread,
What makes you think that it's gone to my head?
No matter what you say, you can't intimidate me
Because I'm the biggest thing that'll ever be.

I've given kisses,
Given hugs,
And sinned so much, I just swept it under the rug,
But I'm not scared
Because I'm still standing here,
Gonna take a lot to make me afraid,
Not saying I'm amazing
But not even wind can blow me away.

Guess I'm the biggest thing since sliced bread,
What makes you think that it's gone to my head?
No matter what you say, you can't intimidate me
Because I'm the biggest thing that'll ever be.

I got famous
And then I lost my fame,
But that never stopped me from being a pretty face,
My mother always says
I look good in a frame,

But that's just her motherly way,
Though I'm quick to give you a nod,
You have my word that
I'm NOT listening at all.

Not a thing you can do
To stop me from passing through,
Ready my podium, ready my lies,
All I need is my suit and tie
And a few gullible minds

Abyss

I stood on the diving board, my steps quick and light,
And I dove into the water, intoxicated by its pretty blue eyes,
But I couldn't see what the others had seen,
Suddenly I was freefalling, suddenly I was free.

Diving into the great unknown, the weak sink fast,
Its brutal tides can knock down even the strongest man,
I opened my eyes and saw its great big monstrous teeth,
Licking its lips, its final course was me.

You can't always trust what you see,
Behind every smile a monster sleeps,
Things looked so pretty, at least I thought they did,
I'm going down into the great abyss.

Cement legs keep me from walking out of here,
Lyin' eyes can fool you but they cry no tears,
Things looked easy; at least I thought they did,
I'm freefalling in the great abyss.

I stood on the diving board with my eyes closed,
I wasn't about to jump unless someone threw me a rope,
But I took that leap and suddenly I was free,
Free from everything that ever bothered me.

Fear hides inside every dream,
Waiting to take advantage of you when you sleep,
I stood on that diving board and opened my eyes
And I took that leap, arcing out wide.

Oceans Away

Fighting a war you never signed up for,
Gone are the days of sunshine and warmth,
Now you're covered in dust on an alien land
And another man's blood stains your hands.

Tucked up your sleeve is a picture of your mom
And written on the back is "I love you, son"
But it's hard to feel loved when you're covered in blood,
Covered in the blood of someone you love.

And you're oceans away from a white picket fence,
Shoulder to shoulder with your brothers in Afghanistan,
You're spending your Christmas on alien shores,
It'll be six more months 'til you're home from your tour.

As the sun sets and the bombing subsides,
You retire to your tent, thankful you're still alive,
You dream of your home oceans away,
Suddenly, a nylon tent just isn't the same.

And you're oceans away from a white picket fence,
Shoulder to shoulder with your brothers in Afghanistan,
Reading your Christmas cards on some barrack floor,
It'll be six more months 'til you're home from your tour.

And you're oceans away from our hearts,
It's gonna take more than tattered flags in our yards,
Flapping like injured birds against the wind,
The stars and stripes get covered in blood time and time again.

Quicksand

Coming out of my barricade,
I'm having a hard time waking up my sleepy head,
Time's got a way of breaking you down,
Like an old warship that's run aground,
Old pieces of leather, tattered and torn,
My tired hands can't turn the wheel anymore,
But words can't describe what I'm feeling right now,
I try and try but I can't get the words out,
I kneel down to tie my shoe
And as soon as I stand up,
My brother's got a bullet-size wound.

What's the plan anyway?
Just old scars that'll never go away,
Something must've slipped in through the cracks,
I didn't notice it at the time but I wish I had.

Childhood aspirations have begun to rust,
Like a toy soldier left out in the mud,
He must've gotten lost behind enemy lines,
I guess something came undone in
The grand design,
Just like him, God's armor never protected me,
It only came apart at the seams,
And I stood there vulnerable, ready to die,
All I had to do was load my gun
And stick it right between my eyes.

What's the plan anyway?
Just old scars that'll never go away,
Something must've slipped in through the cracks,
I didn't notice it at the time but I wish I had.

Blind are a young man's eyes, I was mystified,
I never saw the beauty in things,
Only the black and white,
But when you're kneeling before a white cross,
You come to realize all the beauty you've lost.

Wings

I've got your picture in a frame
Clutched to my heart,
Something to remember you by,
Your name's tattooed on my arm.

Those high school days just flew on by,
Got married and had a kid,
Got deployed to some distant shore
And we haven't seen you since.

Sent off to some foreign land,
Helmet on and a gun in your hand,
Dirt and dust cover your face,
They've given you a number instead of a name,
You're too young to fly; yet they gave you wings,
You're too young to fight; yet you're shooting everything.

Hot Wheels and baseball cards
Traded in for ammunition,
Night sweats and cold shakes,
So they handed you a pension.

Remember your brother,
Remember your friends,
Tattoos on your arm
Of the soldiers who never made it home again.

Home

Sitting on the porch, watching the sun set over the bay,
The sun's setting later and later every day,
And I can smell dinner being made,
It's my home away from home, how I'd love to stay.

Walking along the beach, I see old ruins of a ship,
And I can still hear them yelling as they are about to hit,
And the waves are crashing all along the sand,
It's my home away from home and home is where I am.

It's my home away from home,
I've got everything I need,
A suitcase full of clothes and a windbreaker for the breeze,
'Cause it's my home away from home and home it'll always be.

Lying on the water, the sun's now hugging the sea,
And there's a sailboat captain tacking against the breeze,
And wild horses gather their young to feed,
It's my home away from home and home it'll always be.

It's my home away from home,
I've got everything I need,
A suitcase full of clothes and a windbreaker for the breeze,
'Cause it's my home away from home and home it'll always be.

Sitting on the porch, I see lightning out at sea,
Must be a storm coming in
'Cause the scent of rain hangs in the breeze,
I'm going home tomorrow,
Better pack my bags and memories,
This is my home away from home and home it'll always be.

Americana

Somewhere beyond a white-picket fence,
Somewhere in the south,
Sits an old farmer behind a plow, knocking the cornfields down,
And inside that old farm house, an old woman bakes a pie,
And together, they sit and pray,
Thanking God for their lives.

All the money in the world couldn't buy them happiness,
'Cause as long as they're living here,
Their money's been spent,
And they're hand in hand in prayer, in God they believe
That everything's peaceful as can be.

Somewhere beyond the plow,
Deep in the South,
The congregation gathers for church in the good part of town,
Oh, they're standing hand in hand, praising Jesus for their sins,
'Cause they're working for the Lord,
And they're working for their sins.

All the money in the world couldn't buy them happiness,
'Cause as long as they're living here,
Their money's been spent,
And they're hand in hand in prayer, in God they believe
That everything's peaceful as can be.

Somewhere beyond the farm,
Cornfields grow abound,
And the farmer and his wife pick that corn until the sun goes down,
They're working for the lord, 'cause in him they believe
That everything's peaceful as can be.

Somewhere in the south, the air smells of rain

But the farmer's hard at work sipping on cold lemonade,
His wife's in the kitchen, preparing a meal to eat,
And everything's peaceful as can be.

Loneliest Child

I can hear the words you say,
they tear me up inside,
Behind the door I hide,
I wipe the tears I cry
And dream of a better life.

You used to love me,
So much, so much you did,
Now I'm just a shadow
Of the boy you love to hit.

The loneliest nights
Are nothing compared to you,
Drunk on the couch
But it isn't the bourbon that leaves me bruised.

I sit in the basement,
No T.V. just an old picture frame
With a picture inside
Of a boy who no longer has a name.

Hidden under the stairs,
Cold nights in the dark,
Won't be counting my blessings,
No wish upon a star.

But I dream of being free,
Yeah, that'd be me,
I sit by the window
And wonder what it means?

And the tiny child inside
Still runs and hides

From the man who
Beats him when he cries

This Song Has No Title

There's lightning in your eyes, hastiness under your breath,
The look in your eyes is calm, no hesitation in your steps,
But hidden behind your mask, someone who's afraid,
Someone who's been ridiculed and humiliated every single day

You've always been a quiet child, never talked to no one,
You kept locked inside your room polishing off your gun,
You counted down the days 'til you'd show them all
'Cause you never felt noticed, always got made fun of in the halls,
Well, that won't happen again not while you have a say,
And as you pull the trigger, you watch them casings fall like rain.

A disciplined child raised in a Catholic family,
"God loves you, son," but this he couldn't see,
He began to boil and slowly became withdrawn
And then came the day when he just went off.

The smoke rising from your gun is the smell of success
But that ain't enough for you, no, you close your eyes
And put the gun against your head,
You pull the trigger 'cause
You can't take it anymore,
And we stood there motionless as you fell to the floor.

A disciplined child raised in a Catholic family,
"God loves you, son," but this he couldn't see,
He began to boil and slowly became withdrawn
And then came the day when he just went off.

Back at home, they found a note taped to your door,
It read that you loved your parents
But even they couldn't find a cure.

It said in your file that "you did real well in school,
Always well-behaved, you did what you were told,
You never missed a day and earned perfect scores,"
Try telling that to the victims' parents
As their children are being carried out the door.

Don't You Love Me No More

My, my, what have we here?
A small, innocent child left to die in the cold,
The snow is falling, temperature as well,
Got to be some kind of diplomat from hell
To leave him stranded out here alone,
I guess nobody loves him no more.

A case of heart turned to stone,
Oh, this hatred bruises my bones,
Justice must have been lazy that day,
How could his mother treat him this way?
Only a shadow plays with the toys on the floor,
I guess nobody loves him no more.

Behind the tears, behind the blood,
I find that this boy can still be loved,
I like to believe good exists in every man,
He just finds it hard to hold in his hands,
But when I see that lonely boy
Lying motionlessly on the floor,
I still think nobody loves him no more.

So hard to believe
That someone could treat you so cruel
And stand back and say
They didn't do this to you,
I'd like to look them in the eye
And ask them why?
Have they no heart to hold?
Don't they love you no more?

Heal the Pain

In this room are two lonely people trying to prove
A little love can go a long way,
But their silence is captivating because they don't have much to say,
And through the long sleepless nights of unwanted fantasies,
The past becomes a monster kept in captivity.

How high do you have to climb just to prove you're loved?
Sweet, sweet, unconventionally loved?
There's a devil in every room
And he wears your face to prove
You'll never survive but with my love
You're going to.

Poor lonely child with such timid eyes,
You've seen so much, heard so much,
Enough to make you cry,
Forgiveness burns like an ember on your skin,
But that hurts nothing like seeing the past learn to walk again.

Oh, how high do you have to climb just to prove you're loved?
Sweet, sweet, unconventionally loved?
There's a devil in every room
And he wears your face to prove
You'll never survive but with my love
You're going to.

Close your eyes and drift off to sleep,
Been a busy day, been a busy week,
Where's your father?
Oh, he's been drinking all night and day,
He says he loves you,
But that's not enough to heal the pain.

How high do you have to climb just to prove you're loved?
Sweet, sweet, unconventionally loved?
There's a devil in every room
And he wears your face to prove
You'll never survive but with my love
You're going to.

Been a rough ride most of your life,
But angels pass you by
On every street,
In a passing car,
They hold you wherever you are.

Street Kid

School uniforms and paper airplanes
Took up most of your childhood
But drove you insane,
Now lonely days turn into lonely nights,
Dirty bedroom floor
Covered in used needles and crack pipes

Growing up, locked inside your room,
Curtains drawn
And sadness looms,
There are too many drugs to prove
You're innocent,
A child spent,
You hate living like this,
But you'll take what you can get.

Quiet now,
Such a noisy dog, you're gonna piss your owner off,
And he'll make you spend the night out in the yard,
But he doesn't notice 'cause he's a drunken mess,
And you just carry on, safe and sound,
Succumbed to the bliss

Heavy rain and gusty winds
Blow back your hair as you inject
Your heroin,
You're fine now 'cause you're settled down,
Lying face down on your un-kept bed,
Such a soldier, an honored vet,
Seems peaceful now
But there's still a war raging inside your head.

Quiet now,

Such a noisy dog, you're gonna piss your owner off,
And he'll make you spend the night out in the yard,
But he doesn't notice 'cause he's a drunken mess,
And you just carry on, safe and sound,
Succumbed to the bliss

You stumble upon
Old pictures of you inside an old shoe box,
And you can't help but wonder
Were you ever loved or not?

Jodie

Working late on the bad side of town,
Pouring the sailors their drinks, another round,
Flirtatious eyes when they smile at her,
Jodie blushes like a rose; the boys love their girl,
But it's one more round
And they're singing a broken tune,
One she tries to remember but their words are slurred
And it might as well be mute,
Such a picture perfect moment being drawn in a go,
You would have thought
It was a portrait painted by Van Gough,
Brandi or whisky or whatever they'd like,
She serves them with a broken smile,
No, she won't be leaving 'til
The morning shakes hands with the night.

Jodie lives in the city where the animals run around,
She pays rent with the money she makes on the town,
Her parents are gone; she hasn't seen them in years,
But she cradles their picture dampened by her tears,
Never late for work, she arrives on time,
She's gonna pour her boys their whisky and wine.

Working so late, night and day become the same,
Her emotions are tattered; her hopes are drained,
She has an empty heart, an empty soul inside,
But she doesn't hide her feelings
'Cause they have no place to hide,
Been a rough ride, enough to make a sailor cry,
But she laughs with them, tucking her pain away,
She wears a blank face when the memories remain.

Jodie hands in her tips, she hands in her towel,

Nothing else she'd rather do before her ship runs aground,
She could rule the world but she'd rather serve them rum,
The beauty of an angel, her heart beats like a drum,
So damn perfect, she wouldn't change a thing,
But if she had the choice, she'd ask for a wedding ring,
So many years wasted, she poured them down the drain,
No use in crying 'cause nobody's listening anyway.

She packs her bags,
She's gonna get away from this place,
She loves herself too much to watch her life slip away.

"Goodbye cruel world," she whispers in a labored voice,
She's made up her mind; she's made her choice,
She's waiting for the bus, standing cold in the rain,
Gonna ride away from this life in vain.

Fade Away

Paper hearts and homemade valentines
Turn into broken hearts and a noisy fight,
How could you ever fall in love with a man like him?
How many more times will he hit you before you notice this?
Dirty clothes and a broken smile
Hold you close and they hold you tight.

Lonely eyes in a quiet room
Capture the darkness that you've been looking through,
How could you ever fall in love with a man like him?
How many more times will you overdose before you notice this?
Rent's due but the money's spent,
Sex and drugs don't pay the rent.

Picture frames hold onto the past
But the good ol' days just don't seem to last,
How could you ever fall in love with a man like him?
How many more times will he bruise you before you notice this?
A simple push and the lights go dim,
You close your eyes and you're free again.

Silence breathes inside this room
Disturbing the darkness that's been holding you,
A little push and you're free again,
Fade away, fade away.

Darkness Hides in Every Corner of My Room

Looking back, through old pictures and magazines,
Could have sworn I was Superman
But it was all just a dream,
Back then I was younger, I had my screws on tight,
I was tougher than leather and could win any fight,
But the fire keeps me warm these days
'Cause winter's fierce and it ain't going away,
I need to know that I'm gonna hang on a little bit more,
Sometimes I worry but I just look over to that fire
And I'm secured.

Darkness hides in every corner of my room,
Wearing black like the devil's groom,
Secret eyes watch me sleep,
But at least somebody's watching me.

Intoxicated by high proof blood,
Bourbon doesn't heal the pain
But when I'm pumped full of its sin,
I feel loved,
I've wasted so much time casting shadows on the wall,
But when it came time to admit my mistakes,
I saw nothing at all,
My seclusion's been good company,
Only my shadow notices me,
I need to know that I'm gonna hang on a little bit more,
Sometimes I worry but I just look over to that wall
And I'm secured.

Cold

Driving down Lincoln Way,
Meeting an old friend at Stan's Café,
There we conversed most of the day,
But nothing could have prepared me
For what he had to say

This gentle man took me to a place
Where fear wears an innocent boy's face,
All the words can never explain
This man's heartache and pain,
Just a thirteen year old boy left to die
In a Hungarian prison
With stone-cold eyes,
"Somebody, please turn out the lights;
I don't want to see this hell with my own two eyes,
I'd rather see darkness before I die."

My eyes met with his,
How could God treat a child like this?
The world divided down
A common line,
I too was born in '29.

This timid child fled from home to home,
Nine million people but he was all alone,
A hostile police state under prejudice skies,
"We arrived in cattle cars
And were separated into two separate lines;
Standing six-foot tall with the darkest eyes,
A Nazi guard looked at us and said this line:"

"This is Auschwitz, an early grave,
You will either be gassed or work as a slave,

And if you don't work, you'll be sent to die,
The choice is yours: work or die."

"I froze in fear as we began to march,
Those who couldn't keep up were shot dead on the spot,
But when darkness fell, I broke free,
And pleaded with my friend to follow me,
He declined and we locked eyes,
I later found out that he was killed that night."

The sun was shining as we parted ways,
Amazing how his words took me back to that
Time and place,
Soon before long my old friend will be gone
But his story cannot be lost.

Dedicated to Sam

To Wherever the River Flows

Lately I've been feeling strange
And don't know who to blame,
They say you can still hear the thunder
Even after it rains,
But somewhere down the river's shore
Sits a boat without an ore,
I'd like to sail that river 'til it reaches an end,
The river flows and the river bends.

Don't know what life's given me,
Don't know what it means to me,
Lately I've been searching for
A life that doesn't exist anymore,
But somewhere down the river's shore
Sits a boat without an ore,
I'd like to sail that river 'til it reaches an end,
The river flows and the river bends.

And wherever the river flows,
In my boat I will go,
Don't know what it means to me,
But I know it's somewhere I have to be,
Through the rapids and the waves,
The river carries me away
To wherever the river flows,
Wherever the river flows

Underneath it all is an empty curse
or maybe just a napkin tucked in my mother's purse,
Maybe a tear dried too soon,
Maybe it's our silence being noisy in the room,
But somewhere is the strength to be strong,
So I'm gonna sail the river before the water's gone.

Hard to say if I still believe
In anything that I can't see,
Never been one for spirituality,
Never once did I believe,
But in my boat I will go
To wherever the river flows,
And I'm not coming back 'til I reach its end,
The river flows and the river bends,
The river flows and the river bends,
The river flows and the river bends.

Bridge Over Water

It's a tough world and a tough life,
If you run too fast,
You'll fall on the knife,
Look at the sky,
See God standing there,
He sees you crying
And he doesn't care.

Under a rock sits a man,
He lost his faith
Because he don't understand,
Stole his money
But was there a plan?
Holy Roller must have gone mad,
He feeds on the ones who don't understand.

I'm a man
And my eyes aren't blind,
I have a voice
That gets ignored sometimes,
But all my anger is water under the bridge,
I can't fight the demons that are his.

I don't care
And to think I ever did,
I had a friend
Lose everything that was his,
But don't cry,
Try to understand
That we drown in the blood
That stains his hands

Things Change

It hasn't rained in days
And the riverbed's beginning to show
Its backbone of dirt and clay,
And this family farm is dying,
The corn stocks are withering away
And their prayers go unanswered
As they watch their lives
Buckle under the weight of the pain.

This old family farm is dying,
Drying up more and more each day
And they say they're moving on
'Cause it hasn't rained in days,
It's just a circumstance of ignorance
When God promised that
He'd dry the tears from their eyes,
But these poor souls went unnoticed
And now they've been left to die.

There's sadness in the wind
Blowin' around the dirt,
The graveyard that was once the farm
Has been left to be collected by
The devil's hands,
It's just a circumstance of evil
Left to run amongst the land

But the sad look in their eyes
Says they've given up,
Restless lives turn to stone as
They watch their plow begin to rust,
Guess their tears aren't enough
To heal the ground of its drought,

It's just a circumstance of ignorance
And of a family left in doubt

Reason for Life

Shaping the world with her hands,
Shaping the world
Into something she understands,
The wind and the rain
Shape rocks,
Constantly shifting the sand
And she's the nature that shapes this land.

Mother Nature's daughter,
She has a naïve beating heart,
Raised on whisky, raised on rum,
Her heart beats like a drum,
She's a beauty queen,
She comes to save her city,
Sheds her skin for no pity,
She sees the best in her people.

Cutting the ties that bind,
Her reason, it ain't hard to find,
She sees the best in her people,
She knows they have a reason for life,
She knows they have a reason for life.

A super hero
Flying her way through downtown,
Collecting their pain and suffering,
Absorbing the best of what's around,
She grabs their hands,
So scared are they,
She's gonna heal their pain
And show them the way.

Cutting the ties that bind,

Her reason, it ain't hard to find,
She sees the best in her people,
She knows they have a reason for life,
She knows they have a reason for life.

She believes in a second chance
And she wants to give it to them,
'Cause life's unfair sometimes
But she knows they have a reason for life.

Just Imagine If the Whole World Came Crashin' Down On You

Just imagine if the whole world came crashin' down on you,
What would you do?
Sell your shares to the poorest man?
Tell your kids you love them
And wish them well on their way,
Would you give me your wings and watch me fly
Into that blue, blue sky?
Anyway you put it,
Your chance is now,
Don't wait for that mean old world to come crashin' down.

Just imagine if the whole world came crashin' down on you,
What would it prove?
Would it prove that everything bad happens to you?
Your mother's dying and you kiss her goodnight,
Bet you never thought it'd be a kiss goodbye,
Changed forever, you can't take back the things that you said,
Fighting isn't worth it in the end.

Just imagine if the whole world came crashin' down on you,
Not a Goddamn thing you could do
But dig a hole in the ground, close your eyes,
And see your life from a different side.

Graffiti is electrifying, bloody words of hate,
Carved in stone are the prejudices we can't erase,
What if the world came crashin' down on you?
What would it mean?
What would it prove?
The world spins the same whether you win or lose.

Anomaly

I'm standing on a bridge
Looking down at the water below,
Flowing like a storm
But who knows where it goes,
I've got a factory inside my head
Pumping out all kinds of words,
Some stay inside
And others, they get heard,
I never wanted you to know,
I didn't know how far it'd go,
This water's getting high
And I think we need a boat.

But there's no way around it,
There's no place you can hide,
It's a shape shifting anomaly
That hides inside my mind.

Mother Nature's a monster
With big scary teeth,
She hides inside her cave,
She hides inside of me,
There she waits for stimulus,
She waits for her cue,
Who knows what she'll do
When it gets warm again in
The month of June,
She's a wild animal,
Mother Nature's a mystery,
She's got a wild side to her
And it hides inside of me.

I'm looking at the ruins,

Mother Nature's mess,
I'm sure she didn't mean to do it,
Lord knows she tries her best.

I Am Strong

So many chances gone to waste,
You've let the best of you slip away,
There's nothing more I can do
But show you that it's up to you
To change your life, to smile again,
Because there's only so much
I can do as a friend.

We sat around the dinner table and talked about life,
You told me about yours and
I told you about mine,
Then the tears began to flow as you started to cry,
You told me how much you hated your life,
I held your hand in mine so tight,
And I promised you that everything would be alright.

The world's such a crazy place,
Confusing you, getting up in your face,
You got to be strong and never look afraid,
And I tell you, girl, it's never too late.

Bright eyed and beautiful you have always been,
You have to be strong
And don't let them win,
We sat around that table, staring face to face,
Your eyes revealed everything that made you this way,
Good times and bad times seem to be woven at the seam,
An hour has passed and now you can see.

I've listened to your story
And your merciful plea,
But nothing's gonna change if
You don't listen to me.

Nothing's gonna change if you don't listen to me.

My Sweet Addiction

The hardest part is saying goodbye
To a life I wish I never had,
Just a time in my life when I was difficult,
A time in my life when I was going mad,
I was crippled in confusion
And wrapped up in the delusion
That my horoscope was coming true,
I guess that's what I get for loving you.

The hardest part was when you walked away,
You left me with nothing
But a baggage claim,
I've spent so many long nights knee deep in pain,
Oh, I never thought my life would end up this way,
But this addiction's been my mother,
Holding my hand, telling me which way to go,
It's time I let go of her hand
And find my own way home.

And my life's begun to crumble, piece by piece,
It's just cracks in the pavement
Where you and I used to meet,
A street corner on fire
But I guess it's the lightning in your eyes,
It's been my obsession for most of my life.

The hardest part is the silence
And the shadows on the wall
Creeping up behind me,
They're standing six-foot tall,
It's a horrible situation,
My life's in pieces on the floor,
I guess you're starting a brand new life

And don't need me anymore.

Tenants on the 13th Floor

Early morning rain,
Steady as can be,
But I take it as it comes,
Mother Nature's always after me,
I'm watching my garden grow
From a room of little light,
I can barley read my book,
The one you gave me years ago,
And it feels like a sacrifice
To be living this life
Here on the 13th floor.

Draw the shades,
Turn down the lights,
Poor kids have to play in candlelight,
But it don't bother me anymore,
We'll drink 'til we're sober
Here on the 13th floor.

Having your neck in my hand,
I start living large,
Been doing it for years
Living in the bone yard,
I don't need you anymore,
So stop knocking at my door,
I was born to die on the 13th floor.

I'm lying on the floor,
You pulled the rug out from under me,
Tough love cares enough to
Say I'm in too deep

Been standing in cold water,

It must've been a dream,
So cold are your intentions
But you mean so much to me,
Been living here for years,
The rent's hard to pay,
I'm knee deep in fear
And it won't go away.

Holding myself up against the wall,
Screaming, it'll be okay,
I don't need you anymore,
I wasn't born to die here on the 13th floor.

December

Inside a room sits a wooden chair
And an old mirror with no one there,
Just dead flowers litter the floor
But you can't smell them anymore.

A cold December in the North
And you can't feel your hands anymore,
Sitting in that chair, you're blind to see
That your whole world's crumbling
Piece by piece

Petals and thorns obscure the floor
But you can't feel them anymore,
You can't keep living your life like this,
No one gets a second chance to live.

A dangerous game that no one wins,
The pendulum swings but doesn't miss,
Imagine having to kiss your kids goodbye,
I guess you didn't love them enough to try.

Don't look now but an angel's here
And she's gonna take you away with her,
She's gonna take you to the mother ship,
No one's ready for a day like this,
No one's ready for a day like this.

A thousand prayers laid to rest,
God knows we tried our best,
But the dirty rags on the floor
Remind me of what we're fighting for.

December's gone

And spring has arrived,
New roses have grown,
Beautiful and bright

A Song about New York City

I see kids throwing Frisbee in Battery Park
And street vendors selling balloons on
5th Avenue
Where the drag queens gather at Lips after dark,
Smoky voices sing the blues at
A nightclub called Le Poisson Rouge,
And the taxi cabs paint Manhattan's streets in yellow
'Cause after all the hustle and bustle,
It's a chaotic kind of mellow.

Rockefeller Center comes alive at night,
Filled with Christmas lights and
Skaters on the ice,
The sound of music hangs over me,
Coming from the Jazz Standard on
27th Street,
Oh, this place has got a lot to say,
New York City's my kind of place.

New York City, just some place I've got to be
And when Christmas comes
And snow is on the trees,
She'll look like a Christmas card, an American beauty,
New York City, just some place I've got to be.

And somewhere in Harlem
A gospel diva sings,
She sings songs about New York City
And the soul that it brings.

New York City, just some place I've got to be
And when Christmas comes
And snow is on the trees,

She'll look like a Christmas card, an American beauty,
New York City, just some place I've got to be.

This skyline's so beautiful,
All the steel and concrete
Holding everything together,
Piece by piece,
Queens, Chelsea, Little Italy;
They're just some places
I've got to be.

The Vale of Tintern

Over every stone ruin
Where silence now breathes,
A rainbow hangs over
Every lost soul that fought to be free

Moss collects over everything calm,
Bricks and mortar barely hanging on
And Wales' painted hills of green,
The silent thunder of Tintern Abbey

Over every stone ruin
Where silence now breathes,
Existence echoes still where
The dead Saints sleep.

The sleeping stones of Tintern Abbey
Echo the magnificence that used to be,
The rustling river makes not a sound
On this sacred ground

Oh, and Tintern Abbey's painted hills of green,
Filled with every stone ruin,
The quiet giants of history,
Mankind's first fingerprint etched in every stone,
An archive of the past and everything
We've ever known.

And Wales' painted hills of green,
The silent thunder of Tintern Abbey,
A story still survives along the river Wye,
Silence is its sleepy dream,
The ruins of Tintern Abbey

And its mystical decay,
Colors of purple, buff and grey
Can be seen through the moss,
Not all of its beauty has been lost.

Over every lost ruin
Where silence now sleeps,
A rainbow hangs over
Every lost soul that sleeps beneath

Valencia

Behind closed eyes, I'm standing on a beach
Listening to the waves crash in Valencia,
Suddenly, I'm a bird flying from its tree,
And I'm free, finally free.

Sitting on the dock, I'm light as a breeze
And free as a bird flying from its tree,
Suddenly, I've become one with the sea,
And I'm free, finally free.

And as the day shakes hands with the night,
The sun slowly collapses out of sight,
And suddenly the world is fast to sleep
Leaving behind an unwoven dream in Valencia

As the waves crash along the beach,
I see wild horses running free,
A sense of freedom suddenly made,
And I'm overcome with a change.

How I'd love to dive into the waves
And let the water carry me away to my maker,
To the mossy rocks where the fishermen
Dock their boats;
But far out at sea, I'd let the sun collapse into me
And I'd be free, finally free.

And as the day shakes hands with the night,
The sun slowly collapses just out of sight,
And suddenly the world is fast to sleep
Leaving behind an unwoven dream in Valencia

And as the world falls fast to sleep,

There's a calmness lying on the sea
But silence is broken when I breathe,
And the waves crash around me in Valencia.

Landing on the Moon

The world once seemed so small, innocent and blue,
Life felt like an expensive hotel where I couldn't get a room,
Big bad world never owed me a thing,
But I wanted to be something bigger,
Maybe I could be king?

I wave goodbye as I board my flight,
Don't care if I'm wrong; don't care if I'm right,
I watch beneath me as I am twenty three miles high,
Gone is the ground for my new home in the sky,
All these stars look like New York City's skyline.

Seeing the world beneath me
Makes it hard to breathe
But I know now how it feels to fly
Twenty three miles high in the sky,
But the ice on my wings
Weighs me down sometimes,
Never have I been so much more than life.

Defying gravity, I jump through God's unwoven dream
And I'm flying high where the sky meets the sea,
Once you've seen the moon and the stars
You realize how insignificant you really are.

The most amazing thing is seeing where it all began,
And I know now it means nothing to be a man.

Diary of a Poet

Sometimes I feel that I'm not good enough
And I feel like I'm breaking up,
Like a broken signal on the radio, you can't hear me at all,
Now stand at the window and
Watch me fall from the top of it all.

My ignorance hides in the trees like an enemy
And sometimes I feel like it's watching me,
Don't know what it wants,
Don't know what it needs,
But I feel like it's getting the best of me.

Playing the role as the condescending one with
His finger on the trigger of a loaded gun,
But behind the creativity, the pendulum swings,
And this child can't fly because
He's got ice on his wings.

Inside and out, I have not figured out, and I don't think I ever will,
Because of me, I am farther from the professional I'd like to be,
Sometimes I cast a spell without a wand
But does that make me amazing?
I think not.

I'll never be satisfied with the work I've done
And I'll always be a trigger away from a smoking gun,
Guess my wind doesn't know which way to blow,
No matter how I cast my sail, it never takes me where I want to go.

Part II

Growing Up

Father and Son

Newborn eyes opening for the very first time,
Full of innocence, full of youthful sunrise,
An ocean of blue, deep sea of pure mystery,
Beautiful baby boy looking up at me.
You took your first steps and ran into my arms,
Your smile and laughter keep me young at heart,
Autumn brown hair, tiny hands, tiny feet,
Beautiful baby boy looks just like me.

Farther From Heaven

Sweet baby boy, growing up so fast,
I can no longer hold you in my arms,
Sweet baby boy, barely says a word,
The world is so big
And these years aren't made to last.

Sweet little boy, playing with your blocks,
You're just a product of time like hands on the clock,
You're beautiful,
Sweet, innocent and young,
You're more vibrant than rays from the sun.

Holding you in my arms,
Sweet baby boy,
You bring me laughter and happiness,
You give me joy,
Farther and farther from heaven I seem to have gone
But you lift me up higher than I've ever gone before.

Graceful little stars, sparkling in my eyes,
These are tears that I do want to cry,
You're beautiful, an angel in disguise,
I may not have been there before but this I'd like to try.

Holding you in my arms,
Sweet baby boy,
You bring me laughter and happiness,
You give me joy,
Farther and farther from heaven I seem to have gone
But you lift me up higher than I've ever gone before.

Sweet baby boy,
More than I could ever enjoy,

I love you and I always will.

Everyday Life

I wish I was young again,
Then I could learn about the world again,
Infant eyes opening up to see you cry,
Whatever happened to everyday life?
I wish I could run as fast as I can,
Sit with my childhood friend
And try to catch my breath,
I want to learn to fly, spread my wings real wide,
And see beneath me everyday life.

I wish I was full of it,
I wouldn't want to search for more,
Sarcastic and shy,
I tell jokes, you laugh and cry,
I wish I was more naive,
A child inside,
But we all forget about everyday life.

Now and then we seem to forget
What everyday life really needs?
It needs the child inside to be let out alive
And for us to watch him run free

I wish I could run from pirates,
Jump around my room,
Pretend I was a spaceman, a monkey
On his way to the moon,
I wish I could be a doctor
And heal your boo-boo
Or be a police man arresting you for the things you do,
I wish I could be president, stand before my stuffed animals' eyes,
I would stand there and tell them about everyday life.

What makes us human is everyday life,
But we stand in its shadow and watch it die,
Imagination colors our brains
And in us everyday life will always remain.

Rocking Horse

Growing up in the suburbs
I had a rocking horse,
My daddy loved me enough
To spend his money
When times were tough,
I rocked that thing all day long,
And with a gun in my hand
I felt strong,
He had long hair and polished pine
And that mean ol' horse was mine all mine.

Strolling through town on my death machine
No one dared to bother me,
We robbed a train like Bonnie and Clyde
And we made it home for dinner time,
Bags of loot, filled with gold,
My rocking horse and I are a story to be told.

Gonna ride, ride, ride all day long,
Gonna ride my rockin' horse 'til the sun is gone,
There ain't a train we haven't robbed
And if you see us riding, give us a nod.

Growing up was hard to do,
That mean ol' thing was getting older too,
Daddy promised he'd treat him well
But he gave him away at a yard sale,
I cried so hard when I came home from school,
I couldn't roam the Wild West anymore,
So I stared helplessly at the empty space
And empty too was my face.

When I got older, I was driving home

And saw two kids rocking a horse all alone,
It took me back to when I was young
With my cowboy hat and plastic gun

Old Soul

Ever since I was young
My mother said I was a special one,
I made friends with old folks
And I was always full of love.

I like old music
It has a lot of truth,
'Cause it has a lot to say
Kind of like I do.

And when I was growing up
I pretended I could fly,
Somewhere in the clouds,
In March, I flew a kite.

I'm an old soul living in the present day
And I'll never know from where I came
But this body's got more than bone in it,
It has a whole lot of grit and happiness.

I was grown in the ground
From dirt and clay,
I was made in a factory
And shipped out your way

I'm an old soul living in the present day
And I'll never know from where I came
But this body's got more than bone in it,
It has a whole lot of grit and happiness.

But when I die,
This old soul's gonna stay on
Because even though

I'll be flying,
It won't mean I'm gone.

Christmas Wish

Must've been a dream,
You were standing on a cliff
Watching the tide roll in,
Watching the ships come in,
Mothers missing fathers,
Sons crying on their pillows at night,
Sitting at the foot of their beds
Wishing they'd be home for Christmas time.

I know what you mean,
The pain can cut like a knife,
You hear a sound in the hall
and the floorboards come to life,
So you hide under your sheets
And try not to cry,
You miss him so much,
Bring daddy home for Christmas time.

Your heartbeat sounds like marching feet,
Your eyes so wide and innocent,
Hope God will hear your wish,
You never wanted anything more for Christmas.

Wake up in the morning,
Christmas time once again,
A picture at your side
But it ain't the same in the end,
Pulling back the curtains
Snowing hard outside,
You can't help but wonder
Did God hear your prayer last night?

You hear a voice in the hall,

You're paralyzed,
The greatest gift is seeing him with your own two eyes,
Faster than you can run,
Faster than the speed of light,
You jump into his arms,
He heard your prayer last night.

My Old Friend

Old dog still got some kick left in him,
But you ain't gonna get the same
Action as you did back then,
Throw the ball and watch him kick back his legs,
And he's gonna get that ball
And he ain't ever gonna beg.

We used to roll around in the summer grass
But now the autumn leaves are falling
Where we used to play catch,
Funny how that old dog still sniffs the ground
As if he remembers something
About the ball he used to chase around

Don't know the kind of friend you got
'Til he doesn't chase that ball no more,
And he doesn't wag his tail
When he's sleeping on the floor,
But you can't separate us even if you try,
Because I love him and he's a friend of mine.

Old dog still got some kick left in him
Because every time I throw that ball
He tries the best he can,
Doesn't wag his tail like he did before,
But he still licks my face
When I wrestle with him on the floor

Man he used to run
Fast as a bullet out of Robert Ford's gun,
He'd chase after that ball
And bring it back to me,
Now he can barely turn his tired head towards me.

Don't know the kind of friend you got
'Til he doesn't chase that ball no more,
And he doesn't wag his tail
When he's sleeping on the floor,
But you can't separate us even if you try,
Because I love him and he's a friend of mine.

But my dog's getting old
And there ain't much spring left in his sprung,
Man I'd love to throw that ball
Just to see him run

Silver Screen Pony

Riding into sunset is
Every child's dream,
He's the hero on the silver screen,
With a tilt of his hat
And bullets in his gun,
He's the bandit on the run.

Strolling down some desert highway,
He's breathing in the dust
And stealing the love of so many young boys' hearts,
He's out to rob a train
For its precious cargo and souvenirs
But you'll never see him quiver in fear.

And he'll ride 'til the day meets the night,
He'll pitch a tent in the canyon
And keep warm by a blazing fire light,
For every kid it's a dream
Just to ride with their hero on the silver screen.

Standing in the dust
With a bullet caught between his teeth,
He don't need a bible to dictate what he believes,
Riding like a storm,
An American hero is born,
He's the bandit in their dreams,
He's the slinger on the silver screen.

Ride away
And soon he'll face another day,
The cowboy kid of the west
Riding into sunset,
He's the hero in their dreams,

He's the bandit on the silver screen.

And he'll ride 'til the day meets the night,
He'll pitch a tent along the Rio Grande
And keep warm by a blazing fire light,
For every kid it's a dream
Just to ride with their hero on the silver screen.

Old Oak Tree

When I was young I used to run around
An old oak tree in my front yard,
I was only ten, with a head full of imagination,
We were pirates, doctors and lawyers,
Anything we wanted to be,
And in that yard, in the summertime,
We were wings upon the breeze.

And as I got older, that tree grew taller,
My friends and I grew apart in time,
But compared to that tree, we felt smaller,
Our naïve eyes still looked at that tree,
We smiled and laughed
Because it took us back to when we were birds,
Souls of the world,
We were free with our wings upon the breeze.

And now I'm old, they've cut down the tree
And built a store from the wood of the old oak tree,
Standing in the parking lot, it still takes me back
To when we were pirates, doctors and lawyers,
Just footprints in the sand,
And now I can see children collecting fallen leaves,
'Cause summertime doesn't last forever
And neither do we

Frozen In Time

Misty wooden benches,
Creaky floorboards,
An old abandoned steam engine
Sits idle anymore.

Abandoned train stations are
Decaying power:
An old split-flap display says
Train leaves on the hour.

Train tracks get lonely
The farther they go on,
Sooner than later they rust
But time rides on.

You'll never know what it's like for me

The sun is setting on
Another perfect day,
I'm still alive anyway.

The world's turning
Night turns into day,
And I look at the blood on my hands,
Did I do something bad?
I'm a murderer for destroying the purity I had.

The sun is setting on
Another perfect day,
I lost track of time
Going past me like a speed train,
Solitary confinement,
Lock away the tears,
They don't want to see you cry
But do they know you've been doing it for years?

Oh mother,
You'll never know what it's like for me,
Constantly hiding my face
From the prejudices they portray,
You'll never know what it's like for me.

Sitting by the window,
Letting fresh air in,
Getting kind of stale,
The scent of death lingers a bit,
Nothing else matters,
Gonna read my poetry,
It takes a metaphor to
Define me.

Oh brother,
You'll never know what it's like for me,
Constantly hiding my face
From the prejudices they portray,
You'll never know what it's like for me.

The sun is setting on
Another perfect day,
But I swear to god
I won't let it go to waste,
I'm gonna spread my wings,
Ma, I'm gonna fly,
There's no use in staying here
If it's gonna leave me behind.

Closet Queen

Writing in your diary,
You're gonna spread the news,
Like fire in the grass
On a summer's afternoon,
Storm is brewing,
Did you tell your father yet?
He might just kill you
And have no regret.

Trying on makeup, dancing in mother's dress,
Did you tell your brother or any friends yet?
You closed the curtains,
Pushed the magazines under the rug,
You love to stay up late reading them
And don't come out 'til you're done.

Been hiding it for years,
Only so many know,
You tease them with charades
But how far will it go?
We have to dig deep
Like we're mining for gold,
Why do you leave us guessing?
Do you think we won't love you anymore?

C'mon out you closet queen,
Do you think you can keep fooling me?
Obvious clues keep poking through
But I don't think any less of you.

Stubborn closet door,
You're locked inside,
Been trying to open that sucker

For most of your life,
You kept me guessing
With your loaded gun,
Thought you'd pull the trigger
And you'd be done.

Keep the Faith

You feel like the outcast kid and you feel like giving up
On life and everything in between but I just wish you could see
That you've got family and friends, who care about you,
I know it feels like you're born to lose,
And I know you're shy but that's no place to hide,
You've got to thicken your skin if you're gonna survive
Their ridicule and pain,
But remember, always remember, to keep the faith,
'Cause every punch that flies and every tear that cries
Don't keep it locked up inside,
Just stay cool in the most casual way and keep the faith.

Well, my friend, I've been there before,
And I didn't think I could take it anymore,
The world weighed so much back then,
I fought so hard but never made a dent,
Their mean words created the delusion
That I was weak but I'm only human
'Cause back then surviving was the name of the game
And I did it every day,
I just stayed cool in the most casual way
And you know I kept the faith.

I know it's hard right now
But just take a moment and look around
'Cause you've got the world to prove
And no one can take that away from you.

And you know they'll never change,
But you can't let them define you in any way,
Just stay cool in the most casual way
And keep the faith.

You feel like you can't catch a break
And you don't know how much more you can take,
Well, just keep your head up high
And remember that I was standing in your shoes at one time,
No matter how much blood I bled,
I knew I was just like them,
Standing 5 foot 10, I was a little too thin,
But I stayed cool in the most casual way
And you know I kept the faith.

'Cause back then surviving was the name of the game
And I did it every day,
I just stayed cool in the most casual way
And you know I kept the faith.

Pocket Change

When I woke up this morning
I put a little kick in my coffee,
I put on my cape, ignored how I behaved,
And I was well on my way.

Business proceeds as usual,
I keep wearing the same old face,
Too many problems in this town,
The kind that won't go away,
I'd be lying to you if I said I was calm,
But as long as the voices keep talking inside my head,
I'll be comfortable with the planet I'm living on.

Outside my window is a garden,
I grow love there, the power of life,
I sit in the rain as it washes me away,
The paints I own and on the easel they're thrown,
They're the colors painting my life.
This life is meant to be,
A thousand faces smiling back at me,
A coffee cup with bitch carved in,
This is the life they feared I'd spin.

I am soul: true and brilliantly bland,
I don't notice the world but I notice who I am.

Business proceeds as usual,
I keep wearing the same old face,
Too many problems in this town,
The kind that won't go away,
I'd be lying to you if I said I was calm,
But as long as the voices keep talking inside my head,
I'll be comfortable with the planet I'm living on.

I lie on my bed with an open eye,
I like to see how high I can fly,
My love is a big, brilliant smile,
And my life's an even more brilliant one.

Dedicated to Baba, thanks for a lifetime of inspiration

Funny How It Goes

When you were a kid you put dad's shoes on,
Dreamed of being big, standing tall and strong,
When you were a kid you wore your mother's dress
And walked around the house in your Sunday best

Sitting in the passenger seat of your father's truck,
You wanna be just like him when you grow up,
Wish you could keep this moment in a picture frame
Because then you'd know it would never change

Funny how it goes, gunny how you can't let 'em go,
Funny how much you miss that old pig skin being thrown,
Fourth of July, Labor Day,
Sitting on your shoulders so he could see the parade,
The precious exchange that happened today,
The bond between father and son will never change.

No longer a boy yet barely a man,
He looks confused but tries to understand,
Seems like time has a plan of its own
Now that your son's fully grown

The yard seems empty now,
There ain't a soul around,
An empty house reflects your age,
You just wish some things hadn't changed.

Funny how it goes, funny how you can't let 'em go,
Funny how much you miss that old pig skin being thrown,
Fourth of July, Labor Day,
Sitting on your shoulders so he could see the parade,
The precious exchange that happened today,
The bond between father and son will never change.

Wish you could have written the book on life,
Then you could throw the ball around one more time,
Funny how a father's love for his son never fades,
It never fades away.

Teenage Angst

The leaves on the trees are changing earlier every year
And my Christmas tree's decorated
But the snow's disappeared,
Some call it global warming,
The crazy things liberals say
But no matter their agenda,
I can't deny what's changed.

Standing before my classroom on finals day,
I've studied for hours, overloading my brain,
I've spent my twenty one years
Rewriting my resume,
I guess what I'm trying to figure out is
Who am I going to be someday?

Guess we're growing up, we're graduating soon,
We got tassels on our caps and a lot of angst to lose,
Standing beside my friends,
I see our lives sewn together at the seam,
Time may try to define us
But it will never define me.

And it's a celebration, my liberation,
I'm finally on my own,
But it's been hard to cue
And hard to prove
My prowess is breaking through.

I'm older now and I'm set in my ways
And there isn't a thing that I would change,
Just the other day, I got a call from a friend
That I haven't seen in years,
He's got a family and a high paying job,

He's making so much money
He's scratching backs with the snobs,
But just hearing his voice takes me back to
My High School days,
Funny, how we've let those days slip away.

Looking back now nearly forty years ago,
I stood in the hallway in between periods
And didn't know which way to go,
And now I'm looking back
While rocking in my chair,
Life's simple now but the angst is still there.

The Distance between Here and There

Someone once said to me,
"You can be anything you want to be,"
I could fly if I wanted to,
There was nothing I couldn't do,
All I needed was a simple dream
And the means of
Breaking out of these boundaries

I've had my hand held through troubled times,
But what's gonna happened when
They cut the line?
Am I strong enough to wipe my own tears?
Is this the distance between here and there?

I've found the strokes of life are learning to paint themselves
And now I can do it all by myself,
Don't need your tender hand, just need to know you've cared,
And now I know the distance between here and there.

Growing up isn't hard to do
Just as long as you've got something to prove,
Doesn't matter if you're too big or small,
The strength to be strong is in us all.

Yeah, it's in us all.

Someone once said to me, "you'll be king,"
And "you'll hit every note when you sing,"
But they don't know who I really am:
Just a boy trying to understand,
Oh, I find that everything I fear is
The distance between here and there

I've found the strokes of life are learning to paint themselves
And now I can do it all by myself,
Don't need your tender hand, just need to know you've cared,
And now I know the distance between here and there.

Now I know the distance between here and there,
And it's good to know you've cared.

But it's all just a fork in the road directing me where to go,
And I don't know where I'm going to,
To some place written in my blood down some ghostly avenue.

Old Timers

I spend time with the old timers at the home,
They have no one and no one knows about them,
There's something inside of me that hates seeing them alone,
So I watch over them and I think that they know.

We talked about the Great War and days since then,
We talked about their friends, who never made it home again,
Sometimes they'd connect to the words that I said,
And I knew then that they weren't completely spent.

In such an empty house a story still prevails,
'Cause it's such an obvious truth even if they don't tell,
I've seen old folks try to get back home,
Such a haunting feeling to know that you're all alone,
It's an endless battle fought with the past
Just enough to know that they aren't going back

And the war that they fight
Will always be fought,
But they can never win,
Only admit that they've lost,
It's a shame to see their warship
Go down this way,
A United States marine admiring his final days.

Looking into their eyes is like going back in time,
The rise and fall of great nations, such a cruel life,
Never enough money,
God, those days were tough,
Never knowing if you were going to eat another meal or not,
I spent time with the old timers 'til the day they died,
And I'm sure as hell that I made a difference in their lives.

The Diving Board

Once I was six dreaming to be eight,
I was a gladiator charging from the gates,
Ma always loved me, made me get good grades,
Taught me to be strong and never look afraid,
So I grabbed the rung and swallowed ev'ry fear,
Now I'm standing on top,
And I'm glad to be here.

Climbing up the ladder, the champion I've become,
No place to hide, ain't no place to run,
Standing on the clouds, gonna shout and be heard,
Watch me, ma, jump off the diving board.

Sharks huddled below come to catch their prey,
They ain't getting me; today's not their day,
Running for the edge, this is the best I'll ever get,
No time left to place another bet,
Gonna scream real loud, loud enough to be heard,
Look at me, ma, I'm jumping off the diving board.

Climbing up the ladder, the champion I've become,
No place to hide, ain't no place to run,
Standing on the clouds, gonna shout and be heard,
Watch me, ma, jump off the diving board.

Once I was a seed
Ma, planted in the dirt,
Now I'm flexing my stuff
On the diving board,
Gonna run and jump, now I will be heard,
Look at me, ma, I jumped off the diving board.

Dedicated to my loving parents

Faster Than the Speed of Light
(Graduation Song)

The other night I found an old yearbook of mine,
I started strolling through the pages
Not knowing what I would find,
Someone wrote "I want to be with you for the rest of my life,"
Well it's been twenty years since
And I never found the boy who wrote that line.

I was quickly taken back to my homecoming dance
When I was too scared to tell someone
What I had thought of them,
But the night ended and we went our separate ways
And I don't know where he is to this day.

Hard to say time hasn't been wasted faster than the speed of light,
Gone are the good days, old age has robbed me blind,
So many memories, both good and bad,
But no matter what they are,
They're all I have.

The other day I attended a funeral for my friend,
He was my age,
We graduated in two-thousand and ten,
God and her angels have him now
But no matter how much time passes
He will never have the time that I do now.

Hard to say time hasn't been wasted faster than the speed of light,
Gone are the good days, old age has robbed me blind,
So many memories, both good and bad,
But no matter what they are,
They're all we have.

But now I remember that he had written that line for me
And even though time has left him behind,
That line will die inside of me.

Part III

From the Heart

Where Do I Belong?

Words can't describe how I'm feeling right now,
Feels like I'm burning from the inside out,
I used to feel the wind in my hair,
Now I no longer care,
I used to love you, used to love you so much,
But it feels like you're losing your touch,
Can't seem to let you go,
I'm afraid of being afraid to know.

But the same damn question still resides in my mind,
Is there any true love left for me to find?
My stubbornness is fueled by my insecurities,
Maybe it's who I'll always be.

But after the laughter is gone
And all of my friends have moved on,
Where will I belong?
Oh, where do I belong?

Hope my crying doesn't wake you tonight,
Don't bother calling, I'm gonna be alright,
But these chains wrapped around my soul
Grow tighter the more I lose control,
I grow tired of my friends' advice,
They tried to help me but I'm wound too tight,
Guess I don't know what's right for me,
Guess this is as good as it'll ever be.

I'm getting older and I'm running out of time,
It's so hard to watch my friends move on with their lives,
I can't seem to let these burdens go,
Where do I belong, oh, I don't know.

But after the laughter is gone
And all of my friends have moved on,
Where will I belong?
Oh, where do I belong?

Dedicated to Tiffany

Runaway Train

You left me high and dry
Like rain without its sky,
My identity becomes the breeze
Blowing through the trees,
Standing at a fork in the road
I've got a map in my hand but no direction to go,
I can choose any road I like,
One leads to darkness and one leads to light.

I thought there was a chance
For this to be a fine romance,
But I bit off more than I could chew,
The same can be said for you,
But I know that I am strong
And I will pick up my pieces
And move on,
This will not be my eulogy,
You're gonna see a brand new me.

The train's coming down the tracks,
Screeching to a stop,
And I'm standing in its way
Ready to lose everything I've got,
But I jump at the sight of
Seeing my life flash before my eyes,
I'm not ready to die
And leave everything behind.

Leaving you has left me in a lot of pain,
But I know I cannot win a losing game,
How inviting are the trees
When I'm driving home recklessly,
The whole world feels so unfair

Like nobody cares,
But this won't be my eulogy,
This isn't the end of me.

Behind every storm
The sun shines,
This darkness may be yours
But it won't be mine.

Dedicated to Matt

Desires

I'm a monster in disguise,
If you don't see that then you're bind,
Been a fool at times,
But I never stand back and wonder why.

Keep feeding quarters into the machine,
Stand back and wait for no reply,
I've been out-of-order for some time,
But I never stand back and wonder why.

I'm the victim of the crime
And a martyr at times,
That kind of logic has me scratching my head sometimes,
But I never stand back and wonder why,
No, I never stand back and wonder why.

Desire burns like a shooting star
Passing by you wherever you are,
I get lonely sometimes,
But I never stand back and wonder why.

I'm the victim of the crime
And a martyr at times,
That kind of logic has me scratching my head sometimes,
But I never stand back and wonder why,
No, I never stand back and wonder why.

Crazy intentions running wild
In and out of the fire,
Seems I'm intoxicated by desire,
But I never stand back and wonder why.

Fool For You

I must be crazy
'Cause I don't believe it's true,
And I'd go crazy
If you said you love me too.

I think I'm foolin'
To think you're in love with me
And I must be foolin'
'Cause I know that'll never be.

'Cause every night I pray to God
That he'll make us fall in love,
'Cause when push comes to shove,
Babe, I love you so much.

Oh, babe, I'm a fool for you
And there ain't a thing I won't do
To prove my love for you,
To prove my love for you,
'Cause, babe, I'm a fool for you.

I must be desperate
'Cause like a boomerang, my heart keeps being thrown
And I'm scared
To know the things I don't wanna know.

But I'm a man
And I'm going to hold you in my arms
Someday,
And I'm your man
'Cause there ain't no other way.

But, babe, I'm a fool for you

And there ain't a thing I won't do
To prove my love for you,
To prove my love for you,
'Cause, babe, I'm a fool for you.

I Want You

Something happened on the bridge last night,
The stars were out
And they were shining bright,
We talked about friends and what we did with them,
Then I began to notice how much time's been missed.

Days began to pass, slowly turning into years,
And we lost track of time, we lost track of here,
Just timeless stories, they keep being thrown,
You call them gibberish but I call them our own.

But as time slips away
And people start to change,
The stars begin to fade
And nothing looks the same.

But no matter how much time may pass,
Like sand through an hourglass,
There's still time to lose,
I want you.

'Cause no matter what may be,
It's never gonna be you and me,
I want you.

Something happened on the bridge last night,
It started out as butterflies
But it turned into a bitter fight,
Emotions colliding, both old and new,
I did everything I could to not let them through.

Something in me can't seem to die
And it's slowly becoming the rest of my life,

It breathes and acts just like me,
God, I'd do anything just to be free.

But no matter how much time may pass,
Like sand through an hourglass,
There's still time to lose,
I want you.

'Cause no matter what may be,
It's never gonna be you and me,
I want you.

Feel So Lonely (I Could Die)

I feel so lonely I could die
And I wouldn't even feel it
Because it is my life,
I ask for your advice and you give me space,
I ask for your understanding
And you push me away.

I feel so lonely I could die
But you wouldn't even notice
Because you're blind,
I wish you'd see the blood I bleed,
I wish you'd try to understand me.

Sometimes it takes more than blue in the sky to see how high,
And it takes more than a river to see how much I've cried,
But sometimes I wonder what it's like to fly,
Sometimes I feel so lonely I could die.

They say that happiness resides in us all
But I'm afraid to say that mine might be gone,
I guess there was a crack and everything fell through,
Now what am I going to do?

Sometimes it takes more than blue in the sky to see how high,
And it takes more than a river to see how much I've cried,
But sometimes I wonder what it's like to fly,
Sometimes I feel so lonely I could die.

I feel so lonely I could die,
Go ahead keep on standing there
Acting like everything is alright.

Brothers

I remember staying up late when we were five years old,
We'd tell each other scary stories
'Cause we thought they were cool,
But those days are past me now,
A rusty old jungle gym where we used to play,
Funny, it's summertime
But the leaves have begun to change.

My bitterness has pushed you away
And I'd be lying if I said I'm not to blame,
I just wish I could rewrite the past
And bring you back,
But now we're living separate lives,
Different places, different times,
You and me, we're growing apart
And that's the scar deep in my heart.

There isn't a day that goes by that I don't think of you,
It takes me back to those scary stories we told in our bedroom,
Funny how we were back then,
We didn't care about the trouble we'd get in,
'Cause we protected each other and that made us tougher,
Man, we loved each other.

These memories are all that I've got,
Everything else has been lost
To the monster under the bed,
He'd do anything to see you and me dead.

But the same damn thing still goes through my mind,
I can't help but feel like I'm wasting time
And wasting my life,
Seems we're just an old story that keeps being told:

Two kids tucked in bed, letting their imaginations
Run wild through their heads.

I Forgot To Smile

You're getting married, I am so happy for you,
To the most beautiful girl,
Her smile is brighter than the moon.

You're getting older and so am I, I guess,
But the way you two reverse the world,
There are so second bets.

I haven't felt a rain like this in quite awhile,
I forgot to smile,
But I'm happy for you,
You see, I saw a face in the mirror this morning,
I didn't want to believe it was true.

I've been so far away from reality for awhile,
I forgot to smile.

I love you like a brother, I guess I got ahead of myself,
I made a mess of this occasion,
I trampled over feelings I thought I'd grow to forget.

Everything's been very black and white,
But suddenly things have begun to change
And now shades of grey are taking over my life.

If you're happy, go ahead, take her hand,
I guess there are some things I'll never understand,
The piece of the puzzle remains lost to me,
But this is the best it's ever gonna be.

I love you
But why did it take me a lifetime to say?
I guess I knew it was the answer I just couldn't face.

I haven't felt a rain like this in quite awhile,
I forgot to smile,
But I'm happy for you,
You see, I saw a face in the mirror this morning,
I didn't want to believe it was true.

I've been so far away from reality for awhile,
I forgot to smile.

Two Old Friends (All These Years Gone By)

Looking back now, someone's fogged up the glass
Now I can't see how much time has passed,
It's an illusion, the main express,
Lord knows we can't stop it, lord knows we tried our best
But the laughter and the tears, bad jokes and good cheers,
I can't believe you and me are still standing here.

Looking on, feels like a dream don't you think?
I never knew how much trouble you and I'd bring
But I never cared,
I think it represents us well
And looking on from here,
There ain't a story left to tell.

Looking on from here, just old scars and bones
But the sunset up ahead says we haven't far to go,
Old dust in the wind still blows itself around
Like two kids that won't settle down.

And like the blue in the sky,
No clouds to catch our eyes,
Just to say we tried
And all these years gone by,
Nothing we can do now but
Keep passing through
'Cause we're two old friends with nothing to lose.

Two tired old men converse on their day,
Sitting in their rockers, letting them sway,
Wired eyes connect and the feeling begins,
Nothing beats a moment like this.

Looking up ahead, the glass is still fogged a bit,

But I don't notice it
'Cause our past sticks like a tick,
So many good memories it makes me want to cry,
Friend, I couldn't have asked for a better life.

Dedicated to JJ Marconi

Old Friends Never Say Goodbye

Well, the days are getting shorter and we're running out of light,
All the leaves are changing and so are the times,
Yeah, we're getting older and now that the tide's beginning to turn,
The headlines are screaming watch their futures burn.

Rocking in my chair, humming any tune that comes to mind,
The seasons are changing fast and so are our lives,
You're getting married: a beautiful bride and a handsome groom,
I on the other hand am the same old story you always knew.

But old friends never say goodbye,
They never let each other go,
But the tide turns eventually
And pulls everything out to sea,
Just a moment in my life I wish could stay
But nothing ever works out that way,
No matter how much time passes by,
The past survives
'Cause old friends never say goodbye.

Well, you've got my number and you've got my name,
Funny, your sense of humor has never changed,
Seems our future's turning away with the tide
But old friends never say goodbye.

Looking Through

I was spaced out, I ignored the truth
Standing in front of me cutting through
To the elephant in the room,
Every chance wrapped up in a neat little bow
Handed to you on a silver platter
But you still didn't know,
Sporting perfect hair and a pretty face
Anything to hide how I felt that day,
Every contradiction's a matter of fact
Of who and what I really am.

I was selfish, I was ignorant,
I'm sorry you didn't know that about me back when
We were simply just friends
Naïve to the truth that was lurking around the bend,
But I'm falling apart, piece by piece,
Worried about what you'd think of me,
Just a circumstance of an affair that no one ever saw,
Two shadows dancing up and down the wall.

But I'm looking through,
Observing from a *voyeur's* point of view,
Concealed by the darkness
Trying hard not to be seen by you,
Oh, I'm looking through,
Observing from a *voyeur's* point of view,
Wearing a thin disguise
Trying hard not to be seen by you

I was broken down, I couldn't figure out,
I was tired of starving in the darkness of my doubts,
I was lurking around your life
Trying to control you like a marionette on a wire,

But looking through somebody else's eyes
I now see things from a different side,
The truth hides behind the curtain inside every room,
A voyeur *curiously* looking through

Here Today

I'm looking on,
The conquest of my life
But it still feels cold to me
Like what am I going to be?
Oh, I need you here today,
The monsters under my bed
Are getting inside my head,
Please make them go away,
Oh, I need you here today.

I just need some time undercover,
I need a brother,
Don't need your charity,
I just need you here today,
Oh, with me.

And I need you here today,
I need you here today,
Long nights with the television on
And bad thoughts that I know are wrong,
A noose around my neck,
Beer and a few illegal meds,
I'm working on being saved,
So, I need you here today.
I need you here today.

I'm looking on from yesterday,
Just another page turned
And another lesson learned,
You gave me faith, made me smile,
You gave me strength
For that extra mile,
But things changed

And now I need you here today,
I've been hurt, been bruised,
Oh, I need you
'Cause this world's such a dirty place,
I need you here today.

Saying Goodbye

Driving away in my brand new Cadillac
Our lives are changing fast,
I'll never forget how we were back then,
Somewhere between seven and ten,
I thought we'd always remain as friends
But then again,
This is how our story ends.

We're both going our separate ways,
You're falling in love and I'm coming of age,
Soon you'll be married
And you'll love her with all of your heart
And you'll build a life together as mine falls apart.

And it's hard saying goodbye,
'Cause there's so much I'm leaving behind,
I never thought things would change so fast,
But we both know this wasn't meant to last.

Pictures in an album on my coffee table,
I like to look at them and reflect when I'm able,
Too many memories to be thrown away,
I just can't believe how much has changed,
I still remember when we were twenty two,
Wasting time making time was nothing hard to do.

And it's hard saying goodbye,
'Cause there's so much I'm leaving behind,
I never thought things would change so fast,
But we both know this wasn't meant to last.

We're both going our separate ways,
You've got a job and I've begun to change,

Soon you'll buy a house
And you'll drive a fancy car
As I spend my money down at the local bar.

And I hate saying goodbye,
'Cause I really don't want to leave you behind,
But time goes on and you can't go back again,
And I'm afraid this is how our story ends.

Happy Today

All I can is that I'm happy today,
I never thought I'd feel this way,
All the darkness and the pain
I thought would never go away.

You gave me a shoulder to cry on,
Told me I was right when I was wrong,
You made my bad dreams go away
And all I can say is that I'm happy today.

Yeah, yeah,
I'm happy today.

Through the pain and the heartache,
There's always a shoulder to cry on,
'Cause sometimes I'm not that strong
And I need someone to lean on,
When the weight of the world's in my hands,
I know that you'll understand,
When life gets to be too demanding,
There's always a shoulder to cry on
And there you'll find me
Still standing

It takes a friend to understand
How it feels to have the weight of the world
In my hands,
Just to know that someone's there for me,
You helped me to see it through
And I thank you.

Looking back through my life,
You helped me through the hardest times,

Stood by me and you never complained
And all I can say is that I'm happy today.

Yeah, yeah,
I'm happy today.

Part IV

Love

Candlelit Bedroom

Those hot humid nights get to me sometimes,
Looking back through our wedding album's
Like dissecting a crime,
Your Mona Lisa smile and deep blue eyes
Distracted me from your cynical side,
So we packed our suitcase and boarded our flight,
We flew down to Mexico for the rest of our lives,
Sewn together by heartfelt vows:
I wrote mine for you but yours now feels like
It was written for somebody else.

For every broken heart that littered the floor,
I gave you everything you wanted but you always
Wound up asking me for more,
For every argument that's been nailed to the door
Falling and breaking into pieces as it hit the floor.

My weary eyes and mind take me back to those
Candles flickering in a Mexican wind,
Blowing out one by one as you and I walked in,
You in that lacy dress under a blue Mexican moon,
A candlelit bedroom with a million dollar view

Looking out the window, I count every star that passes by,
Fueled by every question
That's ever been asked by mankind,
I drift in and out of tears wondering what I could've done,
Stampeding through emotions,
Understanding love's like swallowing the barrel of a gun,
And that moon that shines through my window every night
Reminds me of you in that lacy dress
Lying on an unkempt bed amongst a sea of candlelight

My weary eyes and mind take me back to those
Candles flickering in a Mexican wind,
Blowing out one by one as you and I walked in,
You in that lacy dress under a blue Mexican moon,
A candlelit bedroom lit for two.

For every broken heart is a truth unseen,
Hiding behind the heartache and the disbelief
But looking back to that enchanted night,
Intoxicated by the candlelight

My weary eyes and mind take me back to those
Candles flickering in a Mexican wind,
Blowing out one by one as you and I walked in,
You in that lacy dress under a blue Mexican moon,
A candlelit bedroom meant for two.

Intoxicated By Your Love

Well, your pretty eyes and grand disguise
Pulled me in and wrecked my life,
I only wish I'd seen you coming in through
My door,
I only wish I'd learned from what'd happened to
Me before,
But I was blind as any man could be,
Intoxicated by what I wanted to see,
Drowning in your Italian eyes,
Your mysterious moves truly move me.

Well, I only wish I'd listened to my friends
When they told me what was happening,
But I stayed here and let down my guard
And you took everything, you broke my heart
And still I sat there like a fool,
And neglected the golden rule,
I'm never gonna let down my guard again,
No one's gonna break my heart again.

But I can't keep holding on to these emotions,
They've been causing such a commotion,
Controlling me like a marionette on a wire,
You're dancing me on this beautiful fire.

Well, your pretty eyes and grand disguise
Came in and wrecked my life,
A fresh coat of paint and some casual talk
Distracted me from what was going on,
But I was stupid as any man could be,
Falling for you and your seductive company,
Drowning in your Italian eyes,
Your mysterious moves truly moved me.

Every time you and I meet
Something starts happening to me,
A fire ignites inside my heart
And burns like a beautiful star.

Summertime Love

It's paradise just to be sitting next to you
On this hot summer's afternoon,
Open up a beer and kick off your shoes
And lose yourself in me,
Yeah, I want to grow old with you,
And I want you to fall in love with me,
'Cause there ain't a reason why
But I seem to have caught you on my fishing line,
And I think it was the fourth of July.

Fireworks exploding and the sticky humidity,
But we're cool in the grass
'Cause you're lying next to me,
Maybe a little Frisbee in the park or some loving
Underneath the stars,
We can't turn back the clock but we sure as hell can
Make up for what we've lost,
'Cause there ain't a reason why
But I seem to have caught you on my fishing line,
It must've been the fourth of July.

Well summer's gone and September's here
And we're heading back to school,
But I ain't waiting 'til next year to see you once again,
'Cause there ain't a reason why
But I seem to have caught you on my fishing line,
And I think it was the fourth of July,
Funny how time has passed us by

My Rose

You took me by the hand and asked me to dance,
You were a gentleman but I was a mess,
Butterflies came and went but I just closed my eyes
And felt your lips press up against mine.

Silence poured over me as I listened to you breathe
And then you came into me,
Your ocean blue eyes cut through me like a knife,
Cutting through everything, everything inside,
You tore through my vessel, washed me away,
Babe, you took my breath away.

You made it rain when you stole my rose,
And you picked its petals and threw them on the floor
But I didn't need them anymore,
Fixated on your smile and the dimples on your cheeks,
It was the way you looked at me.

You took me by the hand and knocked me off my feet
And carried me into a candlelit bedroom
Made for you and me,
We were in love, your fragile smile and sky blue eyes
Took me to a place where I never felt higher,
My dreams froze like ice the moment
We danced under a thousand blazing stars,
Burning like the fire inside my heart.

You made it rain when you stole my rose,
And you picked its petals and threw them on the floor
But I didn't need them anymore,
Fixated on your smile and the dimples on your cheeks,
It was the way you looked at me.

Your innocent smile and casual design
Fill my heart a thousand times,
Your ocean blue eyes, calm as the sea,
Cut through everything inside of me.

Night Train

It's getting late,
Nine o'clock to be exact,
The last train is leaving,
One by one the passengers let 'emselves out.

Making friends
With shadows on the wall,
I light my last cigarette
And one more drink before last call.

Another night on a suburban train,
Another night watching my love being taken away,
The smoke in the air is thick tonight,
Every cigarette's telling me that I'll be alright,
There's so much I want to say through words unheard,
Please don't go,
I can't help myself anymore.

Sitting at the bar
Putting money in the jar,
Asking the piano player,
Play another sad song for me.

I sip my drink,
So strong, yet light as a breeze,
Dull as the clothes I'm wearing
But it rocks me like the seven seas.

Another night on a suburban train,
Another night watching my love being taken away,
The smoke in the air is thick tonight,
Every cigarette's telling me that I'll be alright,
There's so much I want to say through words unheard,

Please don't go,
I can't take you leaving anymore.

I sit at the bar, a drink in my hand,
I see a reflection in my glass as an old man,
I put out my cigarette, that won't be me,
I won't let the engineer take my baby away from me.

My Blues

I'm in denial about you and me,
I've been too scared to say anything, been hard to breathe,
It's been tearing me apart from the inside out,
Just listen to the words falling from my mouth.

You see, I get lonely sometimes and need someone
But I can't tell the difference between this and love,
So many crazy, contradicting feelings that I've lost count,
Just listen to the words falling from my mouth.

Turn around, look away,
I don't want you seeing me this way,
I've been wrapped up in my blues,
Drowning myself in gin and juice
'Cause I can't face the fact
That you aren't coming back
Anymore

And everybody thinks that I'm going mad,
They tell me to get over it 'cause it ain't that bad,
I'm a caged animal looking through the glass,
Who no one understands, they just stare at me and laugh.

(Always) We Begin Again

Standing on the staircase, I watch you kiss our kids goodbye,
I never dreamed I'd be standing here watching you tear apart our
lives,
Guess this is it, no more warm summer nights in July,
I guess I have to learn to sleep alone in this cold bed
But always, we'll begin again.

Soon enough I'll learn to live again
And before these seven words get said
Know that I will never be the same again,
"I love you and I always will,"
I can't shake these words from my head
But always we'll begin again.

Standing by the window, I watch you as you pull away in tears,
The feeling's mutual, I never dreamed I'd be standing here,
And the kids keep asking me "is mommy coming home again?"
But I just tell them "she loves you," and "we'll begin again."

But you'll never know a pain like this,
Tell me, was it something that I said?
Never knew how fast my heart could run,
God, I miss her so much.

But soon enough I'll learn to live again
And before these seven words get said
Know that I will never be the same again,
"I love you and I always will,"
Why can't I shake these words from my head?
But always we'll begin again.

The years have passed, seasons too,
I never knew how much a man could lose,

But I still love you, that'll never change,
Guess some things just can't be replaced.

I Slow Dance As If you're Still in My Arms

Remember those summer days
Lying together in that Kentucky bluegrass, getting wet in the rain,
A time when I was just starting out, those awkward teenage years
But they never defined us as we watched our innocence disappear.

Driving down the road, counting corn fields in a row,
Your hand in mine, I was your superhero
But when I went swimming in your eyes, in an ocean so blue,
Forever and always was a promise I made to you.

That bluegrass lied down every time it rained
And we rolled like thunder as we watched our lives begin to change
But when I went swimming in your eyes, in an ocean so blue,
Forever and always was a promise I'd never lose
'Cause summer came and went, our fate was written in the stars,
I slow dance as if you're still in my arms,
I slow dance as if you're still in my arms.

From homecoming king and queen to graduation day,
They handed us our diplomas and sent us on our way,
You went off to school and I got a job
But I slow dance as if you're still in my arms.

That bluegrass lied down every time it rained
And we rolled like thunder as we watched each other change
But when I went swimming in your eyes, in an ocean so blue,
Forever and always was a promise I made to you
'Cause summer came and went, our fate was written in the stars,
I slow dance as if you're still in my arms,
I slow dance as if you're still in my arms.

Sometimes I still drive through my old hometown
And wonder what you're doing now,

If only I had the chance to see you in my arms again
Then we'd slow dance together until the world ends.

Strangers in Love

Two awkward lovers
Stand in the middle of a room,
Staring into each other's eyes
Not knowing what to do,
He's seen her before
And she's seen him too,
Down at the market
But now she's in his bedroom.

He didn't know her name
And she didn't know his,
And they didn't know each other
But there was nothing to it,
He asked for her hand
And she quickly gave in,
He looked into her eyes
And she looked into his.

Two strangers in love hold each other close,
Discovering life together, discovering love,
Two strangers in love, a heart like a dove,
Set free from the past, set free is this love.

He closes his eyes
And she closes hers,
She's dancing with him
And he's dancing with her,
Two stones rub together
And a spark ignites,
Two lovers on the run
Discovering life

Two strangers in love

But they're just two kids,
Discovering life together,
Discovering this

Two Idiots in Love

I'm no doctor but I think there's something wrong,
I used to carry my own weight; I used to be strong,
But suddenly I'm weak
'Cause someone needs someone,
But I ain't one of them, I've got no one.

I'm so foolish writing these words down for you,
But I'm not foolin' 'cause these words are the truth,
I'm going crazy and I'm running out of time,
'Cause someone needs someone
And I need you in my life.

Some may say I'm crazy
And others may say I'm mad,
But they don't understand
The kind of man I am,
Someone who wants a hug,
Someone who needs someone,
Frankly, we're two idiots in love.

I think I'm losing my touch, now I'm two steps behind,
'Cause in this race for first place I can't see the finish line,
But I ain't giving up; I've got so much to prove
'Cause I'm not just someone,
I'm someone who's in love with you.

I may be foolish; I may be an utter mess,
But it's these words that have never been harder to confess,
Oh my love, for you is a rose without its buds,
Yeah, we're two idiots in love.

Some may say I'm crazy
And others may say I'm mad,

But they don't understand
The kind of man I am,
Someone who wants a hug,
Someone who needs someone,
Frankly, we're two idiots in love.

And maybe it'll all make sense,
Maybe there'll be a second chance,
Just someone who needs someone,
'Cause I'm an idiot in love.

One Love

Miss Liberty's hands are rusting now
Bleeding her sadness but she doesn't make a sound,
Every broken mother that ever loved us
With her broken heart that feels so out of touch.

The world's so heavy and it's weighing down on me,
Beneath these ruins, love sleeps quietly,
Watch as the dove
Flies like a burning angel high up above,
Searching for something, searching for someone,
One love
One love

Our fathers and brothers marched for us,
They burned the churches and sat at the front of the bus,
But Miss Liberty's hands are rusted now,
She bled her sadness but she never made a sound.

War costs money but love doesn't cost a thing,
The bills are piling up and so is the debt ceiling,
Behind these cold eyes my war rages on,
I'm searching for one love that isn't wrong.

The world's so heavy and it's weighing down on me,
Beneath these ruins, love sleeps quietly,
Watch as the dove
Flies like a burning angel high up above,
Searching for something, searching for someone,
One love
One love

Watch as the dove
Flies with a broken wing high up above,

Searching for some place to land, searching for someone,
One love
One love

You changed the World

I was broken down, I was spent,
I was without a home, you paid the rent,
When my heart was wondering free
You saw the best in me,
I never asked you to do that for me,
So I thank you for changing the world for me.

I was broken, I was broken down,
When times got tough,
You came around
And picked me up from the ground

Oh, I was barely breathing,
I was losing faith,
Hard saying I had any
When everything in my life was crumbling away

But you changed the world,
You changed the world for me,
When I thought I had nothing
And I thought I could never win,
You picked up my pieces and took me in,
And I thank you, I thank you.

I was lonely through nights all alone,
Scared of myself, waiting by the telephone,
You were my guardian angel,
You gave me hope,
You gave me love when I needed it most
And I thank you, I thank you.

Together Again

So much time has passed me now,
You look so damn happy without your old man around,
I'm only human, I make mistakes,
But there are some things I can't change.

I guess Daddy's little girl is growing up
And she's growing farther out of touch,
Sometimes I look through old pictures of you
And wonder if there's anything left for me to lose.

I never knew how many ways my heart could bend
Fighting for your trust again,
I just wish you'd read the letters that I send,
Sending my love to you
And for you and me to get back together again

You never told me what drove you away,
Was it something we both couldn't face?
If you won't tell me then I don't know how I can change,
I never knew a man could feel this much pain.

But no matter what it takes in the end
I hope to find us back together again,
I need you now more than I needed you then,
I hope to find us back together again.

So much time has passed us now,
I hear you got married and bought a house,
But it ain't the same as it was back then
When you told me you loved me time and time again.

You look so damn happy without me around,
I'm one broken heart away from a box in the ground,

But I'll always love you like I did back then
When you told me you loved me time and time again.

Simple World

Believing in a chance was a masquerade,
Two separate hearts just slipping away,
We never touched on issues unbound,
A better life is something we never found.

You took my heart and tore it apart,
Our worlds crumbled and so did the stars,
Our ship's sinking fast in the stormy sea,
The water's not as calm as it used to be.

I thought it was for life,
Two hearts shaped into one
But the tables turned
And now you're gone,
I thought this was love,
Now a broken dream,
I can change but the same can't be said for you,
Some things go unnoticed
From another's point of view.

Suddenly, I'm half the man I used to be,
Don't look at me, you wouldn't recognize me,
Just a shadow of someone you used to know,
But now it's time for me to go.

Watching the world change right before my eyes,
I sit under your shadow and can only wonder why?
Underneath it all hides the bitter truth,
There are so many things I never thought I'd lose.

The Lovers That Never Were

I thought I knew your name as you came and went,
Took my money and you were gone the very next day,
I thought I knew you but we all make mistakes,
I never thought the love I gave would be the love you'd never take.

I rose to the occasion, I dressed under the impression
We would be together for eternity and never look back to say
"What have I done?"
"Who do I love?"
"Who am I?"
I guess there's more to the rain falling from the sky.

I guess we're the lovers that never were,
Just an occasion, a situation, worn out fringe on a rug,
Two lonely people just searching for love: the lovers that never
were.

I had a picture; it withered away as if I never had it at all,
The frame has cracked; very matter of fact, there's no looking back,
To hold you in my arms would give me just enough life
And I'd realize I may have been wrong but to know you weren't
right.

I guess we're the lovers that never were,
Just an occasion, a situation, worn out fringe on a rug,
Two lonely people just searching for love: the lovers that never
were.

Strange Faces

Sometimes I wear a thousand faces
And you don't know who I am,
I hide behind someone different each time
But I promise you that I'm still the same man.

Sometimes I go a little bit crazy,
And I don't know what I need,
I guess I'm afraid of what you'll think of me.

Still, I'm sorry for the time I've wasted,
I never meant to cause you any pain,
I'd do anything just to have you back again,
Honey, I swear I'm gonna change.

And every time that I've broken your heart,
Every time that I went too far,
Sometimes, honey, I go to extremes
But that ain't me,
No, that ain't me,
I just wish you could understand that I'm a man
And I make mistakes sometimes,
But, honey, I swear I'm gonna love you
'Til the end of time,
Honey, I'm gonna love you 'til the end of time.

Sometimes I feel disconnected,
And I make the same mistake,
I feel like a stranger
'Cause my world's being taken away.

Still, I can't shake those old feelings
Hiding inside my heart,
I've tried to cover them up

'Cause they always seem to do me harm.

Through The Long Night

Sitting at the bar, you order another drink,
Your eyes look tired, they don't even blink,
The crowd's winding down, time to go home,
But no matter how full the room is,
You feel so alone.

Spilling your thoughts on me for a while,
You dance around the truth in such a classic style,
Coming up with excuses 'til quarter to four,
Is it that you don't love him anymore?

Through the long night
I'm gonna stay by your side
And you can rest your weary mind
Right here next to mine,
Oh, and through the long night
What are you still fighting for?
Is it that you don't love him anymore?

Sitting on the stool, you look at the clock on the wall,
Suddenly you realize time has stalled,
Everybody's goin' home now and I think we should too
'Cause the bar's no place to drown your blues.

Through the long night
I'm gonna stay by your side
And you can rest your weary mind
Right here next to mine,
Oh, and through the long night
What are you still fighting for?
Is it that you don't love him anymore?

Walking to the car, you lay your head on my shoulder,

Your tears are warm but you never felt colder,
Tell me, dear, what are you still fighting for?
Is it that you don't love him anymore?

Remember, girl, the sun always shines after it storms,
So what are you still fighting for?
Is it that you don't love him anymore?

You're really worth Fighting For

I remember when I was young
Someone cared for someone else,
I remember when I was younger than that,
Someone cared for someone else,
Paper hearts get torn when they're
Handled with angry hands,
And before they're taped back together,
They're let go to the wind
And we never get them back again.

I remember growing up
You promised me nothing would come between us,
But as we got older,
Something came between us,
I guess we may never change
But that's no reason to live in vain,
Oh, it takes the darkness to shed light on the truth,
And it takes the darkness to find you.

And in my soul
I have your heart to hold
Because you're really worth fighting for,
Through thick and thin
And the trouble we've gotten ourselves in,
I'm coming through and protecting you
From the storm you've caught yourself in,
I don't know if we can fix someone that's been so badly torn,
But I know we will
Because you're really worth fighting for

Sometimes we forget where we came from
And we don't accept our prize,
Sometimes we're blind to the truth

Staring us right between the eyes,
Guess we have more in common than we think,
And it pushes us to the brink
Of war,
But I don't want to fight with you anymore
Because you're really worth fighting for

And in my soul
I have your heart to hold
Because you're really worth fighting for,
Through thick and thin
And the trouble we've gotten ourselves in,
I'm coming through and protecting you
From the storm you've caught yourself in,
I don't know if we can fix someone that's been so badly torn,
But I know we will
Because you're really worth fighting for

Seems the clouds have cleared
And you wiped away your tears,
See you don't have to live your life
One day at a time,
Because in this life you have only one shot
To love someone,
But don't ignore them because of the things
You may have done,
Anger and bitterness can shake you at your core,
But I'm gonna let it all go because
We're really worth fighting for.

Now I sleep with an open mind
Knowing that both ends of the world
Aren't so far apart anymore

Always On Your Side

I'm always on your side,
No matter what they say,
No matter the games that people play,
I'm always on your side
For better or for worse,
No matter how bad it hurts,
I'm always on your side.

People are always leaving their inconveniences behind,
Searching for new beginnings,
Out to find a better life,
No not me there's no place left to hide
But behind open eyes,
I'm always on your side.

I'm always on your side,
No matter the sacrifice,
No matter who's wrong or right,
I'm always on your side
For better or for worse,
No matter how bad it hurts,
I'm always on your side.

People are always leaving their inconveniences behind,
Searching for new beginnings,
Out to find a better life,
No not me there's no place left to hide
But behind open eyes,
I'm always on your side.

I'm so happy now,
They can burn this whole town down
And everyone inside,

We'd walk through the ruins together
And find our strength together
And we'd watch our worlds collide,
I'm always on your side,
Babe, I'm always on your side.

Money Can't Buy Me Love

Life on the road's no way to raise a family,
The headlines and the money are ingredients for tragedy,
But no matter how I'm feeling, it's the same in the end,
Your smiling face is always enough to get me back home again,
Maybe it's my child laughing, eyes full of youthful sunrise,
Maybe it's you lying next to me,
Your innocent smile and blue eyes
Creep into every corner of my life and take me by surprise,
The silly things that make me smile,
Something I haven't seen in a while,
But no matter how I'm feeling, it's when I'm lying next to you in bed,
Your smiling face is always enough to get me back home again.

Plane tickets for business trips, cashmere steam-pressed suits,
And a million dreams made on my pillow in every lonely hotel room,
But no matter how much money I make when the day is done,
My heart's won over by you 'cause money can't buy me love.

I've gone down this road a thousand times before,
And I saw the sun rise and set a thousand times more,
But no matter how I'm feeling, it's always the same in the end,
Just the thought of you is enough to get me back home again.

I turn the radio to silence
So I can hear the world around me breathe,
Suddenly I see that open stretch of road
And something comes over me,
Maybe it's the thought of you growing up alone
'Cause I always said goodbye, I never said hello,
Our unspoken silence is a catastrophe,
Selfishness and money are ingredients for tragedy,

I've been down this road a thousand times before,
But I watched myself leave you a thousand times more.

My suitcase and passport camouflage the vagabond
Searching for an answer some place where the light's turned on,
But no matter how I'm feeling, it's always the same in the end,
Your smiling face is always enough to get me back home again.

Have You Ever Loved A Woman?

She's beautiful,
She's young,
She's spring where the most beautiful flowers haven't yet sprung,
Her boundaries are broken and twisted,
She doesn't know what she wants,
But you're an animal at understanding
The how's and why's of true love

Her heart is not a stone to be thrown,
Know when to leave her alone,
If she wants love in her heart, she'll tell you which way to go,
She has her mother's eyes,
You have your father's lies,
You're an animal at understanding how to keep true love alive.

Have you ever loved a woman?
Do you remember her name?
Is she your forever?
Does she wear a pretty face?
She's a girl living in a woman's world,
Respect her choices made,
Be a man and take her heart in a gentle way.

She's so young,
Innocent and true,
Respect her wants
And she'll respect you.

Hold onto her
And don't let her go,
Don't be an animal,
Control how your feelings show.

Have you ever loved a woman?
Do you remember her name?
Is she your forever?
Does she wear a pretty face?
She's a girl living in a woman's world,
Respect her choices made,
Be a man and take her heart in a gentle way.

Love has no boundary,
True love is running free,
Be a man and understand
So she too can run free.

Together Through Life

From the day that we said our vows
To the day that we picked out our towels
From Pier 1,
You said you liked red but I liked green,
So we argued in the car
And we came to an agreement,
We bought the red ones.

From the day that I smashed cake in your face
To the day that we watched our kids play
In the backyard,
It was such a wonderful time,
That was us together through life.

And together through life we learn,
We yell and we fight and it hurts
But that's what love is all about,
Figuring these stupid things out,
Like what color our house should be,
That never really mattered to me.

From the day that we were two naïve friends
Afraid to look at each other,
But all that changed when we held hands,
We looked into our eyes and the fireworks boomed,
And suddenly there wasn't an ounce of fear left in the room,
"I love you" and "I love you too."

And together through life we learn,
We yell and we fight and it hurts
But that's what love is all about,
Figuring these stupid things out,
Like what color our house should be,

You set off the spark in me.

And when the day comes that we get old,
You'll still be the one that I hold,
In my arms you'll gently sway until your last breath fades.

Old Love

Maybe a lover's touch never fades,
That's at least what I heard today,
The words "I love you" clung on to
Every labored breath,
Maybe a lover's kiss never quits
Even after the darkness closes in,
Behind the silent thunder a storm still roars,
But it's gentle as a rose,
A rose without its thorns

Maybe a lover's promise never breaks,
That's at least what I heard today,
A gentle breeze drifted across a crowded room
Carrying a smile and the words
"I love you too,"
Maybe a lover's touch never grows cold
Even as the skin surrounding their soul
Grows old

Maybe the meaning of love never fades
Even after they forget each other's names,
A brain ravaged by a forgetful disease
Never forgets the meaning of love,
Eternity

Maybe love never dies,
Maybe love exists beyond space and time,
Maybe a lover's touch never grows cold
Even as the skin surrounding their soul
Grows old

Part V

Loss

4 AM Flight (Heaven)

She's waiting for her 4 AM, red eye flight
And she's starting to tremble for she's leaving tonight,
Luggage in hand and she's got her heart on her sleeve,
The world's ambiance seems so small and innocent,
Like a penny that hasn't been spent
It feels like life is so insignificant.

The look in our eyes says we've given up
But we're barely hanging on, not knowing what's left of us,
Can't help but wish we could rip that ticket in two,
But by the look in her eyes, she holds no regret,
And I hope the sun shines wherever she descends
And I hope that it never rains there again,
I blow her one last kiss as her plane ascends.

And as she flies away,
I can't help but wonder why there are tears on my face?
Guess I miss her so much,
Guess I wish I didn't rush
This life along,
But I know she's gonna be strong and smiling as
She boards the plane,
And angels will be waiting for her at her designated gate.

Standing up from sitting down, ain't a soul around,
Guess this is the peacefulness she's finally found,
Empty floor,
Don't hear her footsteps anymore,
Now she's walking in a field of dreams,
Somewhere between you and me
And she's finally free, finally free.

And as she flies away,

I can't help but wonder why there are tears on my face?
Guess I miss her so much,
Guess I wish I didn't rush
This life along,
But I know she's gonna be strong and smiling as
She boards the plane,
And angels will be waiting for her at her designated gate.

Now the moon and the stars
Shine brightly wherever you are,
But my heart's content
Knowing you're happy again.

Your Song

I never believed this day would come,
Because of the words you said,
They put me in a place where I feel no harm.
You changed my life in the following ways:
You gave me happiness,
You gave me strength.

A broken bottle with a message in it,
Reads of the journey you've embarked on,
These dirty days are gonna stick like glue,
But through it all
I'm never gonna stop thinking of you.

And the fire burned your heart,
It burned your soul,
We never felt farther from the grasp of control,
The water came in and washed away your life,
But knowing you're in a better place,
Those are the tears of happiness in our eyes.

I never dreamed I'd have to say the word goodbye,
I never thought I'd have to see you like this,
But to get through it,
I'm gonna try.

And the beautiful world still turns,
But without you it really hurts
Me,
I never thought I'd have to say goodbye,
It just seems to me that you're still alive,
I still hear you say hello,
But deep down inside
I know it has to be goodbye.

Into the light, your steps are short in stride,
I know I'm not the only one who hates saying goodbye,
This life's a cold one,
Letting you go so soon,
But in my heart you'll always have a room.

Dedicated to Henry

A Rose without Thorns

There's a thunderstorm up ahead,
I can see it moving in,
The lightning lights up the sky
Like a million fireflies,
Can't you see me standing here?
In the middle of the road
We've walked this far together
Now I'm walking home alone.

I can still hear those words
When you said you loved me
And I'll never be too far away
For me to be able to say
That I love you,
Oh, and I can still hear those words
Like a rose without its thorns.

There's a rainbow up ahead
And it's heading this way,
Like a peaceful southern breeze
Slowly overtaking me,
Can't you see me walking?
I'm walking back home alone
But no matter where you are
You won't have far to go.

Your words comfort me,
They've always set me free,
A bandage for when it hurts
Like a rose without its thorns.

The Ballad of Matthew Shepard

A '45 in his pocket,
Bullet shells tucked up his sleeve,
Don't remember much, just a rough childhood,
And the words "momma, please."

A finger and a thumb,
An empty can of coke and a fifth of rum,
Finger on the trigger is the distance between
Father and his son

Blind eyes see only black and white,
Not the blue in your sky,
What made you beautiful was covered in blood
And left to die,
Thought you were loved
But they took your innocence,
Hung you like a scarecrow on a barbed wire fence.
You never had a chance; no you never had a chance.

Coming out of the closet
So many years gone by,
No one seemed to notice,
The ones who did, they couldn't keep their anger inside.

Mother's arms are empty with lightning filled eyes,
They stare without expression, without tears to cry,
Robotic were his emotions,
The ridicule must have fried his wires.

Blind eyes see only black and white,
Not the blue in your sky,
Ridicule and pain gave you an early grave,
Hard to believe good men could treat you this way

And who knew that yesterday
Was gonna be your last day,
Who knew all the ridicule and pain would leave you this way?

Lighthouse

There's a window to the world beyond our own,
A place where happiness isn't a boomerang being thrown,
And it's always a sunny day, never a chance of rain,
Such a good story, you don't want to turn the page,
How I'd love to fly there maybe when I'm old and frail,
I hope it isn't too soon but you never can tell,
No you never can tell.

I won't forget about the crazy things we used to do,
Our time spent together; love, I won't forget about you,
Anyway you put it we carved our youth in stone,
But some things get broken, stolen; don't let them go.
Deep inside my heart, an angel awaits my command,
He's ready to fly just as soon as I grab his hand.

These clouds aren't heavy enough to cry,
Why do you have tears in your eyes?
Not like we're saying goodbye
Forever,
Place a rose on my grave before I fly away
To where the songbird plays
And the clouds give way to rain
On a sunny day

The setting sun looks like a lighthouse in the sky,
Illuminating my journey, reflecting my whole life,
Suddenly I'm infinity, a speck of sand on the lens
Flying into tomorrow, never looking back again,
I'm never looking back again.

Something More Beautiful Than Before

Soon your petals will fall from your rose
But then you'll grow
Into something new,
Something more beautiful than before,
Still, it leaves you so badly torn.

Soon your petals will fall from your rose
But then you'll grow
Into something new,
A brand new meaning from something old,
And the sun will shine when you're cold.

Soon the rain will wash away your seeds
To some place new you haven't seen,
Some place more beautiful than before,
Still, it leaves you searching for more.

And when this darkness becomes too much
To bare,
You can throw some of it on me, I'm here,
But for every petal that falls from your rose
There'll be a new one that grows
Into something more beautiful than before

Soon you'll have to face your biggest fear
But I'm not the only one who cares,
For every tear that falls is a lesson learned
That you're not the only one who hurts

And when this darkness becomes too much
To bare,
You can throw some of it on me, I swear,
But for every petal that falls from your rose

There'll be a new one that grows
Into something more beautiful than before

And should you get washed away
And nothing looks the same,
I'm making a promise to a friend
That I'll get you back home again

Dedicated to Virginia

Street Corner Angel

Saw your face on the water
As the waves crashed upon the sand,
And I stood there in somber
Holding your ashes in my hands

Tomorrow is my healing,
No remedy will stop the pain,
Like a storm out on the ocean
Coming into the bay

Saw your name in the stars,
Written in the night sky,
Gone are our yesterdays
But not is your life.

And like a bird from my hands
Freedom is defined,
Disappearing into the sky
But never from our lives,
Your name's written in the stars
And they shine brightly wherever you are.

Saw you on a street corner
Just the other day,
We stared at each other intently
And didn't know what to say,
Just an angel on a street corner
Protecting the passerby,
Gone are our yesterdays
But not is your life.

Tomorrow is my healing
But the pain doesn't go away,

Like a storm out on the ocean
Coming into the bay

Part VI

Idol

You're Famous

Has anyone told you how to get there yet?
Funny, you're so young and innocent,
I'll extend my hand to help you along,
But take it fast before it's gone,
Because in the end it's an early grave,
Too many are hurt and turned away.

You can't expect to be built in one day's time;
Magnificence takes patience, practice, and a brilliant mind.
Wait your turn,
You'll be next in line,
Boy, I hope they find the time.

The pressure will be hard to handle sometimes
But then it wouldn't be the perfect life,
You'll want to jump off this moving train
But you can't stop something
You haven't the power to change.

Some will pretend to be your friend
And leave you with nothing in the end,
They'll plant words inside your head
And take them from your mouth before they're said.

You're going places, kid,
But you can never forget
How much you'll sacrifice
But then it wouldn't be the perfect life.

You can't expect to be built in one day's time;
Magnificence takes patience, practice, and a brilliant mind.
Wait your turn,
You're next in line,

Boy, I'm glad they found the time.

Anyone can say they built the bridge to success,
But you crossed it alone
Just don't let it go to your head.

Dedicated to Shane

Broadway

You wake up in the morning and think about life,
Hard to handle when your name's in lights,
But you open a bottle of aspirin, anything to kill the pain
And you're out the door ready to play the game.

Each step is light, don't wanna wander too far
Because the success you need is right where you are,
Falling tears collect before your tired feet,
You've walked so far and now you're where you need to be.

This city's alive,
Boy, it's calling your name
From the time you step out of the taxicab
'Til you're standing on the stage,
The butterflies in your stomach won't go away,
But your tap shoes shine like diamonds on Broadway.

Dreaming of all the fortunes that fame can bring,
All you have to do is look good and sing,
Your face is all over the magazines
And your name's written on every marquee in New York City.

The hands on the clock move faster now
And so does your name in this town,
From one stage to the next, you're selling out shows everywhere you
go,
You're a household name; you're every teenage girl's hero.

Ticking

Ticking, time is ticking, time's ticking fast,
Deadlines keep getting closer
But success doesn't last,
It only lasts long enough to drive you mad.

No fame and fortune's worth this overkill,
The next big hit's written in a flash,
But I don't know how much longer
I can keep going on like that.

Ticking, time is ticking, time's ticking fast,
Businessmen and their contracts,
Limousines and hotel suites,
The rock star life never sleeps.

Yeah, I make the young girls cry,
And I make the talk show hosts laugh,
But I don't know how much longer
I can keep doing that.

Looking back on my life
I've signed a million autographs,
But now my name's disappeared,
Yeah, I ruled the charts once but I no longer care.

Looking back on my career
I wish I could still hear them cheer,
But I've let it all go
And soon I too will disappear.

Deep Blue Wonder

Seems you've reached an end,
I heard it was hard and it must've been tiresome,
But you mustn't be afraid
Standing alone on the stage,
Oh, I've read your bio in the Daily News,
"A young boy rises to fame
With everything to prove,"
It was the leading story on the front page,
And now you're a New York Times bestseller
Standing on the streets of
L.A.

And sink or swim,
No matter the dirty water you get yourself in,
The award ceremonies, paparazzi,
And the celebrity stories on TMZ,
You've got to watch your every step,
Any one may be that one you regret,
For us to see
Every breath that you breathe,
With our ears against your door,
Your life is now on the diving board.

And it's a lot to swallow, a leap of faith
Jumping off the diving board into this basket case,
Not knowing what is down below,
The deep blue wonder of the great unknown

Seems you've reached the point in your life
You can barely tell the difference between
Black & White,
Oh, you thought they were your strongest suit,
But if you can't tell the difference

Then it's no use,
You've just discovered that the world ain't so small
Anymore
Now that your life's on the diving board

And it's a lot to swallow, a leap of faith
Jumping off the diving board into this basket case,
Not knowing what is down below,
The deep blue wonder of the great unknown,
In the end, will you sink or will you float?

Teenage Idol

Hollywood's got monstrous teeth
Waiting to devour you from
Behind the weeds,
Its bright lights and scandalous ways
Will draw you in
And paint on you a pretty face,
Its façade is bleak but
Looks squeaky clean
Just like those teenage idols
You see on the television screen.

That Hollywood light's really outta sight,
Those stars and planets sure shine bright,
A teenage idol on top of it all
But too soon the stars shatter
And they fall.

All the stars eventually come crashing down,
Breaking into pieces as
They hit the ground,
Your name's been replaced on the marquee
And they cleaned the newspapers
Off the streets,
The teenage idol that you once were
Has no meaning anymore.

You still get played on the radio
Now and then
On oldies stations for has-beens,
Now you're just a flash
From a picture
Taken long ago
When you were a teenage idol

And the world was your throne

That Hollywood light's really outta sight,
Those stars and planets sure shine bright,
A teenage idol on top of it all
But too soon the stars shatter
And they fall.

You're making ends meet by earning tips
Playing covers at
The Holiday Inn,
Sold-out crowds of businessmen in suits,
Watching you make a fool out of yourself
In the back of the room
Playing requests from
8 p.m. 'til 2.

Part VII

Forward

Time

Time has a way of slipping away,
It leaves you with nothing
But the cold embers that were once a burning flame.
The hands on the clock, a constant fight,
Past meets present, they stare each other down with
Cold, unforgiving eyes.
Time has a way of playing games,
Though it's not human,
It reminds you each year of your age,
Cold, unforgiving, and sometimes blunt,
Time is everything that you are not.
Time has a way of robbing us blind,
As soon as we understand it,
We give up and die,
But we accept this as a simple fact,
We learn to live our lives
And to never look back.

Happy Birthday Poem

Love builds a bridge from my heart
To you,
Love is a bandage that heals all
Wounds,
From me to you, a gathering of sorts,
Know this celebrations is truly yours,
Love holds us together in times of
Pain,
Love keeps us together when we stand in the rain
And can't see a thing,
From us to you, one thing stays same,
Today is your day to celebrate.

I wish I could have been there when you learned to walk,
I wish I could have been there when you learned to talk,
I wish I could have been there when you hurt enough to cry,
Because then I could say I didn't let the years pass me by.

The world stops to listen to the song we sing
Of happy birthday and a rap of memories,
Both old and new,
Ones you'd like to kiss and forget,
Anyway, anyhow,
The red carpet is rolled out this way
And let us sing a song of happy birthday.

Surrounded by family, friends and foe,
Reflecting on the tears, fears and so
Many precious moments are weaving their seams
To become the greatest birthday memory,
Happy Birthday

Diesel Engine

The trails I've blazed and the paths I've made
Have become overgrown in my later days,
All these weeds and the smell of kerosene
Seem to be affecting me,
I guess I'm getting old and I'm lost in the fog,
Been driving this old diesel engine
For far too long

My fuel delivery isn't quite like what it used to be,
My parts are rusting and are beginning to overheat,
And the compression and combustion is
Burning me from the inside out,
I guess this old diesel engine's finally breaking down.

Seems my bells and whistles are corroded now
And my pistons are making such an eerie sound,
Kind of like a graveyard gate in an old ghost town,
That's just the sound of this old diesel engine
Breaking down

The small towns and landscapes have all become the same,
Whether it's the Great Divide or
Nebraska's amber plains,
The Northern Star doesn't shine as brightly as it did before
But the thought of getting home strikes the perfect chord.

Seems my bells and whistles are corroded now
And my pistons are making such an eerie sound,
Kind of like a graveyard gate in an old ghost town,
That's just the sound of this old diesel engine
Breaking down

All the places I've seen, I think I've lost count,

Wasn't it Chattanooga, Tennessee where they fought for the south?
General Sherman covered so much ground
But I'm sure his engine eventually broke down.

The Kids Are Getting Older

Two crazy kids out to earn a dime
Selling lemonade in the summertime,
Two broken smiles pave the perfect road
'Cause nobody knows what we
Already know
Just a random chance that we'd met,
Crossing common paths by accident,
Finishing each other's sentences,
Making random things connect,
It takes a fool to make it all make sense.

And it isn't hard to see
what's come of you and me,
Just a circumstance of getting older
And a little bit bolder

But we can see what's written on the wall,
Some too big, others too small,
My naïve eyes don't want to see the truth
Staring back at me and you,
Just a circumstance of going our separate ways,
I never intended for things to change
But I can't keep going down this foggy road,
I've got to let you go,
I know that I've got to let you go.

No it isn't hard to see
what's come of you and me,
Just a circumstance of getting older
And a little bit bolder

And for every time that we went fishing
And yours was bigger than mine,

We just laughed about it the whole way home
Never realizing we were running out of time,
It's these sentimental moments
On the side of the road
That I see as I'm walking home.

Labor Day Parade

Early morning autumn, no rain on my parade,
I can hear the whistle blowing, today is Labor Day,
Summer's over, no more seersuckers worn in high society,
Funny, that kind of thing no longer bothers me.

As fireworks explode in the evening sky,
Another summer is waving us goodbye,
The humidity hangs like a leaf in the breeze,
Funny, that kind of thing no longer bothers me.

And after the parade is done
And the fireworks are gone,
We'll reconvene again
But for now I'm moving on,
The sun is setting on the last perfect day,
Summer has come and gone
And the wind begins to change.

As the night closes in on another Labor Day parade,
I pack up my lawn chairs and retire to my estate,
Been a good life, would not have changed a thing,
If you haven't noticed, it's in the songs that I sing.

Labor Day is over for now anyway,
We'll reconvene again some other day,
Balloons in the air, confetti on the streets,
These are the last of our memories.

Spaceman

A rocket to the moon, anywhere but this place,
Sitting in my room, playing a lonely game of charades,
How I'd love to drop the act and start all over again,
But it takes a lifetime of discovering to see what you could've been.

But this place ain't my home,
I've got so much farther to go,
To my place in the sky where the darkness meets the light,
My immortality's the space between
And it's somewhere I have to be.

Shooting like a bullet through the atmosphere,
Farther and farther I've become from the things I fear,
A step in the right direction,
I'm floating, anti-gravity,
Just my arrogance and beliefs are left to die inside of me,
Left to die inside of me

But I can never go back home,
I don't belong there anymore,
This space has filled my emptiness,
I'm never going back home again.

An astronaut in space,
Watching the anthill I call the human race,
So busy and unforgiving,
Only here do I see there's no meaning to the word
"Living"

And now I'm light-years away from the world I'd like to be,
'Cause landing on solid ground just isn't enough for me,
It just isn't the place I need to be.

A Little Faith

Time has stripped me of my youth
Straight down to the bone,
My tears have dried up with the years
And now I've got nothing left to show.

Time has stripped me of love
Straight down to my core,
The darkest part of living's wondering
What am I living for?

It takes a little faith for it to all make sense,
But it still leaves me weary in the head,
It takes a prayer and something to believe
To find that everything isn't as big as it seems

Life can be demanding,
Yeah, we all feel overwhelmed at times,
But you don't need a prayer
To find an answer in the sky

It takes a little faith for it to all make sense,
But it still leaves me weary in the head,
It takes a prayer and something to believe
To find that everything isn't as big as it seems

This life's a cold walk home alone
Down the darkest road,
Yeah, we all feel lost sometimes
But you don't need a light to find an answer in the sky.

Through The Years

Everybody's got a dream
But too often it seems
That there's a fork in the road
And you don't know which way to go.

And as we last embrace
And everything begins to change,
Tomorrow is today,
Through the years time's a souvenir.

Count your blessings,
Count your scars,
They're souvenirs of all you've been through,
Keep them close to your heart.

Everybody's movin' away,
No one stays in one place,
I guess that people change,
The smiles and the tears,
Laughter and good cheer,
They're souvenirs of graduation day.

Everybody's got a dream
But too often it seems
That everybody moves away,
I guess no one stays in one place.

How about a toast?
One last cheer before you and I have to go,
A glass of champagne, a glass of beer,
These final moments are my souvenirs.

And after everything has changed

And everyone has moved away,
After we're are no longer here,
I'll still have my souvenirs.

After All These Years

I've been lost lately,
Standing in the darkness of this time,
Searching for an answer
That's been so damn hard to find,
Well, I can't say I've found it,
I'm hardly ever satisfied,
Drowning in this moment
That's been so damn hard to define.

I've been lonely lately,
Standing in the darkness of my life,
Searching for somebody,
But I find I'm only wasting time,
Phone numbers carved into paper
Tucked into my pocket,
I can't say I'm satisfied,
I'd like to close this heart of mine
And lock it.

Well, you know I ain't made of steel,
Behind this face is someone who no longer feels
Anything anymore,
So, what's all the fighting for?
Yeah, I'm packing my bags and headin' out of here,
'Cause after all these years, I no longer care.

I've been searching lately
For some kind of truth,
It's been hiding behind the lies
Told by you,
Well, I won't admit that these have been
Wasted days,
But when they're all I've got,

I find I can't complain.

Untitled II

Poetry's just how you were feeling at the time:
Never change anything!
Even if you think it doesn't sound right.
Short phrases and words sometimes rhyme
But they don't have to all of the time,
It's a collection of happiness, sadness and fear from deep inside the heart,
Carved into paper and left for the reader to pick apart.

ABOUT THE AUTHOR

Joseph J. Gombita has been writing poetry for several years. He is currently attending Penn State Greater Allegheny and is completing his degree in Public Relations. He lives in Irwin, Pennsylvania. This is his first volume of poetry.

Made in the USA
Charleston, SC
19 May 2014